SO-AQI-861

DISCARD

Bridges to Reading
Grades K-3

DISCARD

+372.41 BAR

Barchers. Suzanne I.

Bridges to Reading, K-3

Bridges to Reading Grades K-3

Teaching Reading Skills with Children's Literature

Suzanne I. Barchers

1999
Teacher Ideas Press
A Division of
Libraries Unlimited, Inc.
Englewood, Colorado

Dedicated to Judie Eidson with appreciation
for our friendship in Delta Omicron

Copyright © 1999 Suzanne I. Barchers
All Rights Reserved
Printed in the United States of America

No part of this publication may be reproduced, stored in a retrieval system, or transmitted, in any form or by any means, electronic, mechanical, photocopying, recording, or otherwise, without the prior written permission of the publisher. An exception is made for individual librarians and educators, who may make copies of activity sheets for classroom use in a single school. Other portions of the book (up to 15 pages) may be copied for in-service programs or other educational programs in a single school or library. Standard citation information should appear on each page.

TEACHER IDEAS PRESS
A Division of
Libraries Unlimited, Inc.
P.O. Box 6633
Englewood, CO 80155-6633
1-800-237-6124
www.lu.com/tip

Library of Congress Cataloging-in-Publication Data

Barchers, Suzanne I.
    Bridges to reading, grades K-3 : teaching reading skills with children's literature / Suzanne I. Barchers.
    ix, 201 p. 22x28 cm.
    Includes bibliographical references and index.
    Contents: [v. 1] Grades K-3 -- [v. 2] Grades 3-6.
    ISBN 1-56308-758-8 (v. 1). -- ISBN 1-56308-759-6 (v. 2)
    1. Reading (Elementary) 2. Children's literature--Study and teaching (Elementary) I. Title.
LB1573.B3573 1999
372.41--dc21   99-10209
                                                                        CIP

Contents

AUG 0 8 2002

Contents

Contents

How to Use This Book

Teaching reading requires a variety of strategies and interventions, and teachers often struggle to reconcile the mandates of those who advocate direct instruction on basic skills with those who prefer teaching with children's literature. *Bridges to Reading, Grades K-3: Teaching Reading Skills with Children's Literature* bridges those teaching preferences. Drawing on the skills activities found in a variety of basal readers, I compiled a list of reading skills that students should learn in grades kindergarten through three. Using this list of basic skills, I developed activities that use a variety of teaching strategies and discussion options. Many of the activities integrate other subjects such as writing, geography, and oral delivery.

Each lesson is set up in a similar format. A book is identified and summarized for use in teaching a particular skill. A lesson follows that may involve creating a chart to analyze elements of the skill, leading a discussion, or pursuing further research in the library. A list of related books provides titles that may be used to replace the featured title or may be used for further exploration; most of the activities can be easily adapted to another book.

Every effort has been made to ensure that all featured books are still in print. Most of the books were published in the 1990s or are award-winning titles or classics that stay in print. Some books have been re-issued and have multiple copyright dates. Use your interlibrary loan services to obtain books that are out of print.

The organization of the book is an arbitrary alphabetical listing of the skills. Some skills have activities for both grades K–1 and grades 2–3. Others, such as those teaching the letters of the alphabet, are designated for grades K–1. Topics beyond the grasp of K–1 students have activities only for grades 2–3. Teachers of remedial reading might find grades K–1 activities ideal for older students. Conversely, teachers of younger, gifted students might find activities for grades 2–3 to be appropriate.

An underlying motivation for compiling this resource is to encourage the use of children's literature for instruction. Therefore, teachers should not dissect a book so much that the beauty of it is lost for the sake of teaching a skill. Short books can stand up to repeated readings for a variety of purposes. Longer activities can be stretched out over several days to ensure that the students do not tire of the material.

Be absolutely certain that you are comfortable with the content of the book before you read it aloud to the class. I have noted a few instances where a book, such as one that includes ghosts, may be questionable in some environments. Only you can determine the suitability of a selection, however.

As you use the activities, you will undoubtedly recall favorites of your own that might better suit the skill lesson. Be sure to record any substitutions or lesson enhancements for later use. I hope you enjoy integrating reading skills with children's literature.

From: Bridges to Reading, Grades K–3: Teaching Reading Skills with Children's Literature. © 1999 Suzanne I. Barchers. Teacher Ideas Press (800) 237-6124.

 Bond, Michael. *Paddington Bear and the Busy Bee Carnival.* Illustrated by R. W. Alley. New York: HarperCollins, 1998.

Grade levels: K–1.

Paddington Bear and Mr. Gruber go to the carnival and decide to enter the Busy Bee Adventure Trail contest. The goal of the contest is to identify the greatest number of objects that begin with the letter B. Paddington almost loses the contest to someone who has eavesdropped as he compiled his list. But then he remembers one last *B* word—bear!

Activities

1. Read the book aloud, then return to the book and write all the *B* words on the board. Look around the classroom. What other *B* words could you add to the list?

2. Choose another letter for an Adventure Trail. Take a walk around the neighborhood and identify as many objects beginning with that letter as possible. Record them while on the walk.

3. After returning to the classroom, list the words on the board. Have each student copy at least one word onto a piece of white construction paper. Then have the students illustrate their words. Collect all the illustrations and create a cover for a book of words.

4. Challenge the students to repeat the process with a letter of their choice in their house. Have them bring their list of words to school on a designated day. Compare the lists of the students. If time allows, have the students illustrate their word lists.

5. For a variation, have the students create a list of words from *A* to *Z* drawn from objects they find in their neighborhood or home.

Related books

Hague, Kathleen. *Alphabears: An ABC Book.* Illustrated by Michael Hague. New York: Holt, Rinehart and Winston, 1984.

Isadora, Rachel. *City Seen from A to Z.* New York: Trumpet, 1983.

Johnson, Crockett. *Harold's ABC.* New York: Trumpet, 1963.

Kitamura, Satoshi. *From Acorn to Zoo and Everything in Between in Alphabetical Order.* New York: Trumpet, 1992.

Alphabet

Musgrove, Margaret. *Ashanti to Zulu: African Traditions.* Illustrated by Leo and Diane Dillon. New York: Dial, 1976.

Grade levels: 2–3.

This alphabet book begins with *Ashanti*, the word for weavers who make cloth called *kente*. Each page features a letter of the alphabet, a key word, and discussion of the related African tradition. The rich illustrations make this a particularly enjoyable book to share.

Activities

1. Read the book aloud, taking two or more periods to complete the reading. Share the map at the back of the book that shows the location from which each word derived.

2. Discuss how this type of alphabet book provides rich information about Africa. Have the students explore one or more of the books from the "Related books" section below. Choose a topic that relates to the current curriculum. Give each student one or more letters to research as they create a group book on the assigned topic. Have the students illustrate the book, using illustrations from the Internet if possible. Assemble the class book when each letter is ready.

3. Create an alphabet poem, drawing on key elements of the information the students gathered in their research. Write the letters of the alphabet vertically on the board. Then have the person who researched *A* provide three to five words for the first line. Continue with the rest of the alphabet.

Related books

Mullins, Patricia. *V for Vanishing: An Alphabet of Endangered Animals.* New York: HarperCollins, 1993.

Pallotta, Jerry. *The Dinosaur Alphabet Book.* Illustrated by Ralph Masiello. New York: Trumpet, 1991.

———. *The Yucky Reptile Alphabet Book.* Illustrated by Ralph Masiello. New York: Trumpet, 1989.

Paul, Ann Whitford. *Eight Hands Round: A Patchwork Alphabet.* Illustrated by Jeanette Winter. New York: HarperCollins, 1991.

Pratt, Kristin Joy. *A Walk in the Rainforest.* Nevada City, Calif.: Dawn, 1992.

Ressmeyer, Roger. *Astronaut to Zodiac: A Young Stargazer's Alphabet.* New York: Crown, 1992.

Updike, John. *A Helpful Alphabet of Friendly Objects.* Photographs by David Updike. New York: Alfred A. Knopf, 1995.

From: Bridges to Reading, Grades K–3: Teaching Reading Skills with Children's Literature. © 1999 Suzanne I. Barchers. Teacher Ideas Press (800) 237-6124.

From: Bridges to Reading, Grades K–3: Teaching Reading Skills with Children's Literature. © 1999 Suzanne I. Barchers. Teacher Ideas Press (800) 237-6124.

Chwast, Seymour. *The Alphabet Parade.* San Diego, Calif.: Harcourt Brace Jovanovich, 1991.

Grade levels: K–1.

A parade comes to town in this wordless picture book. This parade is unusual because all the participants appear in alphabetical order. Join the spectators and watch the alphabet parade go by.

Activities

1. Share the book by slowly turning the pages while the students study the pictures. Ask them to think about all the letters of the alphabet they see. Write the letters on the board as the students identify them.

2. Discuss how the letters appear in alphabetical order, starting with *A* at the beginning of the parade. Share the book again, and this time have the students identify all the *A* words they see on the first page. Write them on the board. Then continue through the alphabet. (This may take more than one session to complete.) When finished, check in the back of the book to see how many alphabet words the students correctly identified. (There are more than 300!)

3. Using 3 x 5 cards and the word list in the back of the book, print each of the first four words from each letter of the alphabet on individual cards. You will have 104 word cards total. Make up four sets of complete alphabet cards. Mix up each set and place it in an envelope. Divide the class into four groups. Give each group an envelope. Have each group put the collection of word cards in alphabetical order. This can be either a competitive or a noncompetitive activity. Rotate the sets of cards through the four groups so that everyone practices alphabetizing each of the four word lists.

Related books

Kitamura, Satoshi. *From Acorn to Zoo and Everything in Between in Alphabetical Order.* New York: Trumpet, 1992.

Owen, Annie. *Annie's ABC.* New York: Trumpet, 1987.

Whatley, Bruce, and Rosie Smith. *Whatley's Quest.* Illustrated by Bruce Whatley. New York: HarperCollins, 1994.

Alphabetization

Cushman, Doug. *The ABC Mystery.* New York: HarperCollins, 1993.

Grade levels: 2–3.

A work of art has been stolen and it is up to Detective Inspector McGroom to solve the crime. Beginning with the stolen art (the letter *A*), each letter leads the detective to the solution until he can sleep (*Z*).

Activities

1. Read the mystery aloud, telling the students to listen carefully for words beginning with every letter of the alphabet.

2. Write the letters of the alphabet on the board. Beginning with *A*, ask the students to tell you what key words were used in the story. Reread the story to confirm their choices.

3. Work with the students to write an alphabet mystery using the same format as the book. Brainstorm items starting with *A* that could be stolen: apples, antlers, antennae, and so forth. Once the students compose a sentence that works, write it on the board. Keep adding to the story. Have each student take one of the sentences and copy it on the bottom of a piece of white construction paper. When all of the sentences have been assigned and copied, have the students illustrate their pages. Put the book together and keep it in the class library.

4. Challenge your students to create their own alphabet mysteries, letting them work in pairs or small groups. Share these with the class.

Related books

Johnson, Crockett. *Harold's ABC*. New York: Trumpet, 1963.

Kitamura, Satoshi. *From Acorn to Zoo and Everything in Between in Alphabetical Order*. New York: Trumpet, 1992.

Rourke, Linda. *Eye Spy: A Mysterious Alphabet*. New York: Trumpet, 1991.

Whatley, Bruce, and Rosie Smith. *Whatley's Quest*. Illustrated by Bruce Whatley. New York: HarperCollins, 1994.

From: Bridges to Reading, Grades K-3: Teaching Reading Skills with Children's Literature. © 1999 Suzanne I. Barchers. Teacher Ideas Press (800) 237-6124.

From: Bridges to Reading, Grades K–3: Teaching Reading Skills with Children's Literature. © 1999 Suzanne I. Barchers. Teacher Ideas Press (800) 237-6124.

Baer, Gene. *THUMP, THUMP, Rat-a-Tat-Tat.* Illustrated by Lois Ehlert. New York: Harper, 1989, 1991.

Grade levels: K–1.

A parade comes marching down the street with pounding drums and squawking horns. The flutes, drums, and brass become louder, and the figures become larger as the parade approaches. As the parade recedes, the sounds become softer and the figures become smaller.

Activities

1. Practice reading the book aloud before sharing it with the students. Decide where you will increase and decrease the volume of your voice to correspond with the approach and departure of the band. Before reading the book aloud, ask the students if they have ever gone to a parade. Discuss the effect of a band as it approaches and recedes.

2. Read the story aloud to the students without sharing the pictures. Ask the students if they could tell when the band was approaching. Then, read the story again, this time sharing the pictures with the students. Discuss the relationship between what they can see and what they hear.

3. Read the book again. This time, have the students read it with you, starting and ending softly and reading loudly in the middle of the story.

4. Use rhythm instruments or create homemade instruments using Eddie Herschel Oates's *Making Music: 6 Instruments You Can Create* (see the following "Related books" section). Have half the students re-create the parade while the others listen. Can they play softly while approaching and receding? Trade roles and let the others try to replicate the sound of a parade passing by.

Related books

Grossman, Bill. *The Banging Book.* Illustrated by Robert Zimmerman. New York: HarperCollins, 1995.

Oates, Eddie Herschel. *Making Music: 6 Instruments You Can Create.* Illustrated by Michael Koelsch. New York: HarperCollins, 1995.

Walter, Mildred Pitts. *Ty's One-Man Band.* Illustrated by Margot Tomes. New York: Macmillan, 1980.

Conrad, Pam. *Animal Lullabies.* Illustrated by Richard Cowdrey. New York: HarperCollins, 1997.

Grade levels: 2–3.

This collection of lullabies includes poems about the giraffe, alligator, squirrel, oyster, beaver, swan, prairie dog, sea horse, monkey, and owl. But don't be fooled by the title. Not all of these lullabies make the listener yearn for sleep; the beaver's lullaby includes slaps and "whackums!" and the alligator threatens to eat you alive! Large illustrations enhance the poems.

Activities

1. Read aloud one of the poems, such as "Oyster Lullaby," that contains made-up words. Ask the students to listen for unusual words and discuss how and why the poet might have chosen those words.

2. Read aloud "Squirrel Lullaby." Write the little squirrel's response on the board. Have the students read the little squirrel's part. Then have a volunteer read the mother's part while the class responds.

3. Read aloud "Beaver Lullaby." Discuss the use of onomatopoeia with *slap* and *whackum.* Write the first two lines of the lullaby on the board. Have the students read those lines when you cue them while you read aloud the balance of the poem.

4. Divide the class into small groups of four or five students per group. Allow each group to choose one poem to prepare as a choral reading. The poems that have the mother or child speaking a part provide the most obvious division of choral reading. Allow the students time to polish their presentation of the poems and then share them with the rest of the class.

Related books

Brown, Margaret Wise. *Little Donkey Close Your Eyes.* Illustrated by Ashley Wolff. New York: HarperCollins, 1959, 1987, 1995.

Carpenter, Mary Chapin. *Dreamland.* Illustrated by Julia Noonan. New York: HarperCollins, 1996.

French, Vivian. *A Song for Little Toad.* Illustrated by Barbara Firth. Cambridge, Mass.: Candlewick Press, 1995.

From: Bridges to Reading, Grades K-3: Teaching Reading Skills with Children's Literature. © 1999 Suzanne I. Barchers. Teacher Ideas Press (800) 237-6124.

From: Bridges to Reading, Grades K–3: Teaching Reading Skills with Children's Literature. © 1999 Suzanne I. Barchers. Teacher Ideas Press (800) 237-6124.

 Wellington, Monica, and Andrew Kupfer. *Night City.* New York: Dutton, 1998.

Grade levels: 2–3.

Summary: Beginning at bedtime, the city comes alive. Dancers practice at 7:00. At 8:00 weary travelers arrive at their hotel. Workers clean office buildings at 9:00. Each hour of the night is described through text and colorful illustrations until the neighborhood diner begins serving hungry people at 7:00 in the morning.

Activities

1. Ask the students what they are doing at 7:00 at night. Inquire about several following hours. Then ask them what they think happens in the city when they are sleeping each night. List their ideas on the board.

2. Read the book aloud, taking time to appreciate the illustrations and descriptions of the city life.

3. Write "7:00" on the board and see if the students can recall what was happening in the story then. Continue through 7:00 in the morning. Return to the book to fill in any details the students may have missed.

4. Go through the book again and note the activities of the mice on each of the pages. What other animals might students expect to see out at night?

5. Next, have the students create an hourly time line of what they would like to do if they were allowed to stay up all night.

6. Display the students' time lines on a bulletin board entitled, "What We Would Like to Do at Night."

Related books

Carle, Eric. *The Grouchy Ladybug.* New York: Thomas Y. Crowell, 1977.

Crews, Donald. *Night at the Fair.* New York: Greenwillow, 1998.

Kamish, Daniel, and David Kamish. *The Night the Scary Beasties Popped out of My Head.* New York: Random House, 1998.

Fanelli, Sara. *My Map Book.* New York: HarperCollins, 1995.

Grade levels: K–1.

Through simple illustrations, Sara Fanelli has created a collection of maps that categorize a variety of topics, for example, "my day," "my dog," "my tummy." Each map uses a variety of words to label the features on the map.

Activities

1. Share the entire book of maps, discussing the words used to illustrate the maps. Limit this first experience to the sharing of the book.

2. At another time, choose a few of the more simple maps to explore more fully. The map of "my family," for example, would be a good beginning activity. Read the words describing all the family members on the map. Then brainstorm a list of all the words that would work as family members, writing them on the board. Have the students use drawings and the words to make their own family maps.

3. To relate the book to a short lesson on nutrition, discuss the map of "my tummy." Have students list all the foods they ate during the past 24 hours. Then have them map their tummies.

4. Think of new categories and challenge the students to create maps for them. Possibilities include the classroom, a mouse's house, the interior of a refrigerator, a closet, an attic, a mountain, or a desert.

Related books

Aliki. *My Visit to the Zoo.* New York: HarperCollins, 1997.

Cole, Henry. *I Took a Walk.* New York: Greenwillow, 1998.

Dorros, Arthur. *Abuela.* New York: Dutton, 1991.

Zolotow, Charlotte. *When the Wind Blows.* Illustrated by Stefano Vitale. New York: HarperCollins, 1962, 1995.

From: Bridges to Reading, Grades K-3: Teaching Reading Skills with Children's Literature. © 1999 Suzanne I. Barchers. Teacher Ideas Press (800) 237-6124.

From: Bridges to Reading, Grades K–3: Teaching Reading Skills with Children's Literature. © 1999 Suzanne I. Barchers. Teacher Ideas Press (800) 237-6124.

Markle, Sandra. *Creepy, Crawly Baby Bugs.* New York: Walker, 1996.

Grade levels: 2–3.

This informational book sparkles with full color, close-up photographs of baby bugs. Topics include "starting life," "getting bigger," "growing up," "on their own," "taking care of baby," "tricky babies," "home alone," and "becoming an adult." The simple text and clearly labeled photographs make this an irresistible resource.

Activities

1. Share this book by section, exploring the opportunities for classification in each section. For example, in the section on "Two ways to start life," discuss how all baby insects develop eggs, but that their care then differs. Note the body parts on the aphid as well.

2. In "Two ways to grow up," compare the insect babies that eat with those that don't and the presence or absence of wing buds.

3. A particularly fascinating photograph is that of the baby wasps emerging through a caterpillar's exoskeleton on page 12. Classify their life start with the insects previously studied.

4. On page 18, the green tree ants and oakblue caterpillar support each other. Research other insects that have a symbiotic relationship.

5. Once you have fully explored the book with the class, decide on a number of classifications for comparison. Return to the text and photographs and create a chart that contrasts the various baby bugs.

Related books

Darling, Kathy. *Arctic Babies.* Photographs by Tara Darling. New York: Walker, 1996.

———. *Rain Forest Babies.* Photographs by Tara Darling. New York: Walker, 1996.

Fleischman, Paul. *Joyful Noise: Poems for Two Voices.* Illustrated by Eric Beddows. New York: Harper & Row, 1988.

Murphy, Stuart J. *The Best Bug Parade.* Illustrated by Holly Keller. New York: HarperCollins, 1996.

Simon, Seymour. *Wild Babies.* New York: HarperCollins, 1997.

Wisniewski, David. *The Secret Knowledge of Grown-Ups.* New York: Morrow, 1998.

Grade levels: 2–3.

Wisniewski reveals and describes a variety of facts underlying the standard rules imposed on children by adults. For example, children are told to eat their vegetables not because they are "good for you" but because years ago vegetables ruled the earth. Eventually, humans learned to defend themselves against them with weapons and fire, finally conquering them. Each secret is revealed with fanciful illustrations and zany information.

Activities

1. Read the first section aloud, in which Wisniewski discusses his belief that the reasons behind the various rules are "poppycock." Use the various words that the students may be unfamiliar with, such as *macabre, sinister,* and *poppycock,* to stimulate a discussion about the meaning of this section. Then study the illustration. What can the students conclude from the silhouetted pictures of the man running away? Why do they think the text is presented on torn paper?

2. Read the six-page section for "Grown-Up Rule #31." After reading it, return to the text at the beginning that discusses the break-in of the office of the American Produce Council. Do the students realize yet that the disguised eggplant is the author of the book? If they don't understand this device of using a disguise, continue to point it out with each rule until they realize the connection.

3. Read the first two pages about "Grown-Up Rule #37." Ask the students to predict what the truth is behind the rule. Accept any reasonable responses. Continue this process through the rest of the book, comparing their ideas with those of the author. Be sure to take ample time to examine the detailed and clever illustrations, discussing how they contribute to the understanding of the text.

Related books

Perry, Sarah. *If....* Malibu, Calif.: J. Paul Getty Museum/Children's Library Press, 1995.

Wood, Audrey. *Bright and Early Thursday Evening: A Tangled Tale.* Illustrated by Don Wood. San Diego, Calif.: Harcourt Brace & Company, 1996.

From: Bridges to Reading, Grades K-3: Teaching Reading Skills with Children's Literature. © 1999 Suzanne I. Barchers. Teacher Ideas Press (800) 237-6124.

From: Bridges to Reading, Grades K–3: Teaching Reading Skills with Children's Literature. © 1999 Suzanne I. Barchers. Teacher Ideas Press (800) 237-6124.

Day, Alexandra. *Good Dog, Carl.* New York: Simon & Schuster, 1985.

Grade levels: K–1.

In this almost wordless picture book, the mother leaves her baby home in Carl's care. Carl, a surprisingly humanlike dog, and the baby begin a series of adventures that include typical investigations: playing with jewelry and raiding the refrigerator. But Carl returns order to the house before the mother's return, receiving praise for being such a good dog.

Activities

1. Share the book with the class, encouraging them to look carefully at the pictures to see what is happening in the story.

2. Go through the book a second time. This time, ask the students to describe what is happening in the pictures. Ask the students why they think Carl fosters these adventures.

3. Ask the students to speculate on why the mother leaves the baby alone with a dog. Is that wise? Discuss the possibility that Alexandra Day uses this premise to set up an entertaining story line.

4. On another day, return to the story again. This time, have the students decide what the words should be if a simple story line were added. Write the words on large sticky notes. Add them to the bottom of the pages and read the book again. Does the addition of the words enhance the story?

5. Read a variety of other "Carl" books. Repeat the process of determining the story by reading the pictures. Add text and read the new versions aloud. Can the class think of other "Carl" adventures?

Related books

Day, Alexandra. *Carl Goes to Day Care.* New York: Farrar, Straus & Giroux, 1993.

———. *Carl Makes a Scrapbook.* New York: Farrar, Straus & Giroux, 1994.

———. *Carl's Afternoon in the Park.* New York: Farrar, Straus & Giroux, 1991.

———. *Carl's Birthday.* New York: Farrar, Straus & Giroux, 1995.

———. *Carl's Christmas.* New York: Farrar, Straus &Giroux, 1990.

Comprehension: Inferential

Hamilton, Martha, and Mitch Weiss. *Stories in My Pocket: Tales Kids Can Tell.* Illustrated by Annie Campbell. Golden, Colo.: Fulcrum, 1996.

Grade levels: 2–3.

This collection of 30 folktales is organized by level of difficulty for the beginning to advanced young storyteller. Users will find both old and new tales to sample, with directions for telling the stories given alongside each story. General tips for telling stories are also provided for both adults and children.

Activities

1. Choose a variety of stories to read aloud that have a message. For example, in "Bracelets," the girl wants so many bracelets for her birthday that her greed gets her in trouble. Read the story and the ask the students what lesson they could learn from her experience.

2. Read aloud "The Brave but Foolish Bee." Discuss the use of Aesop's fables to tell about political events in a disguised fashion. What message do the students think the teller was giving in this story? Can they think of a political situation with a ruler that prompted this story?

3. Choose four or five stories that have a strong narrative order. Photocopy each story and cut up the story portion into four or five chunks. Divide the class into four or five small groups. Give each group an envelope with the parts of one of the stories enclosed. Have the group decide how the story parts should fit together. Let them confirm their choices with the book when done. Discuss the messages of these stories.

4. Encourage the students to choose a story to tell, using the directions provided. Then suggest they elaborate, using other stories as they become accustomed to storytelling.

Related books

Caduto, Michael J. *The Crimson Elf: Italian Tales of Wisdom.* Illustrated by Tom Sarmo. Golden, Colo.: Fulcrum, 1997.

MacDonald, Margaret Read. *Peace Tales: World Folktales to Talk About.* Hamden, Conn.: Linnet Press, 1992.

———. *Twenty Tellable Tales: Audience Participation Folktales for the Beginning Storyteller.* Illustrated by Roxane Murphy. New York: H. W. Wilson, 1986.

From: Bridges to Reading, Grades K–3: Teaching Reading Skills with Children's Literature. © 1999 Suzanne I. Barchers. Teacher Ideas Press (800) 237-6124.

From: Bridges to Reading, Grades K–3: Teaching Reading Skills with Children's Literature. © 1999 Suzanne I. Barchers. Teacher Ideas Press (800) 237-6124.

Ford, Miela. *Watch Us Play.* New York: Greenwillow, 1998.

Grade levels: K–1.

Lion cubs want their mother and father to watch them play, just like children do. They roll on their backs, touch their toes, play peek-a-boo, tease each other, tickle each other, play tag, and share a stick. Finally they are done, but they want their parents to watch one more activity: taking a nap.

Activities

1. Use sticky notes to conceal the simple text from the students. Read aloud the title of the book and discuss how children like for parents to watch them play.

2. Begin showing the photographs. Ask the students to tell you what they would write for the text, keeping in mind the topic as presented by the title. Record the students' sentences on chart paper.

3. Go through the book a second time. Read each student-created sentence. Then remove the sticky note and read what the author wrote. Discuss the simple language the author used to interpret the photographs. Are the students' interpretations equally valid?

4. Read the text aloud again. Have the students act out each of the lion cubs' actions.

5. Compare this book with Miela Ford's other book, *Mom and Me* (see the "Related books" section below). Can the students interpret those pictures in the same fashion?

Related books

Darling, Kathy. *Arctic Babies.* Photographs by Tara Darling. New York: Walker, 1996.

———. *Rain Forest Babies.* Photographs by Tara Darling. New York: Walker, 1996.

Ford, Miela. *Mom and Me.* New York: Greenwillow, 1998.

Day, Alexandra. *Frank and Ernest.* New York: Scholastic, 1988.

Grade levels: 2–3.

When Mrs. Miller goes away, she hires Frank, an elephant, and Ernest, a bear, to run her diner. They decide to learn the language used in diners. Apple pie and a glass of milk translate to "Eve with a lid and moo juice." When Mrs. Miller returns, she praises their work. This book is ideal for teaching the use of figurative or idiomatic language in a specific setting.

Activities

1. Ask the students if they have special names for foods that they eat. Students may think of *PBJ* for peanut butter and jelly, *black cow* for chocolate milk, *ants on a log* for celery stuffed with peanut butter and raisins, or *monkey tails* for bananas dipped in melted chocolate and then frozen. Make a list of all the names they think of. Discuss how these represent certain foods.

2. Read the story aloud. Then, reread it, discussing how the unique food phrases possibly developed. Discuss how it is necessary to read this story without making literal interpretations but to instead understand it from a figurative point of view.

3. Make a list of all the foods the students have eaten in the past day. Challenge the students to think of creative ways to describe them. For example, a bowl of cereal with milk might be called *boats afloat.*

4. Make up a menu using the new phrases for the foods. Plan a week's worth of snacks or have a breakfast in class using only the new descriptions for the foods.

Related books

Day, Alexandra. *Frank and Ernest on the Road.* New York: Scholastic, 1994.

Elting, Mary, and Michael Folsom. *Q Is for Duck: An Alphabet Guessing Game.* Illustrated by Jack Kent. New York: Clarion, 1980.

Juster, Norton. *Otter Nonsense.* Illustrated by Eric Carle. New York: Philomel, 1982.

From: Bridges to Reading, Grades K–3: Teaching Reading Skills with Children's Literature. © 1999 Suzanne I. Barchers. Teacher Ideas Press (800) 237-6124.

Cole, Joanna, and Stephanie Calmenson. *Yours Till Banana Splits: 101 Autograph Rhymes.* Illustrated by Alan Tiegreen. New York: Morrow, 1995.

Grade levels: 2–3.

This collection of rhymes includes a wide variety of examples of figurative language. The rhymes and sayings are organized by topic, such as friendship, graduating, getting married, things to write when you can't think of anything, and the ubiquitous "Roses Are Red" rhymes. This is an especially useful title to share at the end of the year, when students are signing autograph books.

Activities

1. Begin by examining the book's cover. Ask the students if they see the joke in the illustration as it relates to the title of the book. (The banana is "splitting," or leaving, the scene.) Explain that often such sayings can have double meanings. Turn to page 34 and share the "Yours Till . . ." examples. Also share the illustrations on the pages. Then discuss how they could illustrate a variety of the examples: soda popping, bacon stripping, butter flying. Illustrate the sayings and any others that the students can find.

2. Share the section on page 60, "May Your Life Be . . . ." Discuss the comparisons. Then brainstorm other examples. If necessary, give the students these starters:

    May your life be like an ice cream cone—
    May your life be full of fun—
    May your life be like a flower—
    May your life shine just like gold—

3. Create autograph books to serve as mementos for the year. Have the students record positive rhymes or sayings in each student's book.

Related books

Morrison, Lillian. *Best Wishes, Amen: A New Collection of Autograph Verses.* New York: HarperCollins, 1989.

———. *Yours Till Niagara Falls: A Book of Autograph Verses.* New York: HarperCollins, 1990.

Opie, Iona, and Peter Opie. *I Saw Esau.* Cambridge, Mass.: Candlewick Press, 1992.

From: Bridges to Reading, Grades K-3: Teaching Reading Skills with Children's Literature. © 1999 Suzanne I. Barchers. Teacher Ideas Press (800) 237-6124.

Pfeffer, Wendy. *What's It Like to Be a Fish?* New York: HarperCollins, 1996.

Grade levels: K–1.

Learn where fish live, how the fish's body is suited for swimming, the purpose of scales, how fish use their tails, how they breathe, how they eat, about their body temperature, and if they sleep. Finally, learn how to set up a goldfish bowl.

Activities

1. Before reading the book, share the following anticipation guide with the students, asking them to answer if they think the statement is true or false.

---

1. _____ People can swim better than fish.

2. _____ A common goldfish can have five different kinds of fins.

3. _____ Fish scales are covered with slime, which helps them glide through the water.

4. _____ Fish don't need oxygen.

5. _____ Fish flakes may contain ground-up flies.

6. _____ Big fish don't eat little fish.

7. _____ Fish are warm-blooded.

8. _____ Fish never stop moving.

9. _____ Fish never close their eyes.

10. _____ Sunlight can be too bright for fish.

---

2. Read the book aloud. When finished, return to the anticipation guide. Reread the statements and discuss if they are true or false. What fish facts surprised the students?

3. Make a list of all the kinds of goldfish mentioned in the book. Compare their likenesses and differences.

From: Bridges to Reading, Grades K-3: Teaching Reading Skills with Children's Literature. © 1999 Suzanne I. Barchers. Teacher Ideas Press (800) 237-6124.

From: Bridges to Reading, Grades K–3: Teaching Reading Skills with Children's Literature. © 1999 Suzanne I. Barchers. Teacher Ideas Press (800) 237-6124.

Related books

Dokken, Kay. *Will a Clownfish Make You Giggle? Answers to Some Very Fishy Questions.* Illustrated by Vicki Marcellan-Allen. New York: Aqua Quest, 1995.

Esbensen, Barbara Juster. *Sponges Are Skeletons.* Illustrated by Holly Keller. New York: HarperCollins, 1993.

Jenkins, Priscilla Belz. *A Safe Home for Manatees.* Illustrated by Martin Classen. New York: HarperCollins, 1997.

Pallotta, Jerry. *The Underwater Alphabet Book.* Illustrated by Edgar Stewart. New York: Trumpet, 1991.

Dokken, Kay. *Will a Clownfish Make You Giggle? Answers to Some Very Fishy Questions.* Illustrated by Vicki Marcellan-Allen. New York: Aqua Quest, 1995.

Grade levels: 2–3.

Readers of this entertaining question-and-answer book can learn about clownfish, queen angelfish, parrotfish, jellyfish, a lemon shark, a fiddler crab, a blue-ring octopus, a ridley turtle, pistol shrimp, squirrelfish, porcupine fish, and sea horses.

Activities

1. Choose one of the sea creatures from the book to share with the class. Ask the question posed in the book. Have the students speculate on why the sea creature got its name.

2. Ask the students what they know about the animal and write the facts under the heading "What I Know" on the board or on chart paper. Then ask students what they want to know and record that information under the heading "What I Want to Know."

3. Read the two pages of information aloud and share the illustrations. Tell the students that you are going to read the text again and that they are to write down at least one detail while they are listening. For example, they might write down where the sea animal lives or how it got its name.

4. Share what the students have written. Compare their details with those in the text for accuracy. Add their information to the chart under the heading "What I Learned."

5. Ask students what they still want to know. Write these questions under the heading "What I Still Want to Know."

6. Use the library to locate additional information about the sea animals examined in class. Repeat the process with other sea animals described in the book. Alternatively, assign sea animals to small groups of students and have them continue the research process independently.

From: Bridges to Reading, Grades K–3: Teaching Reading Skills with Children's Literature. © 1999 Suzanne I. Barchers. Teacher Ideas Press (800) 237-6124.

Related books

Fine, John Christopher. *Big Stuff in the Ocean*. Golden, Colo.: Fulcrum, 1998.

Knapp, Toni. *The Six Bridges of Humphrey the Whale*. Illustrated by Craig Brown. Niwot, Colo.: Roberts Rinehart, 1989.

Martin, Kim. *Giants of the Sea*. New York: W. H. Smith, 1988.

Pallotta, Jerry. *The Underwater Alphabet Book*. Illustrated by Edgar Stewart. New York: Trumpet, 1991.

Pechter, Alese, and Morton Pechter. *What's in the Deep? An Underwater Adventure for Children*. Washington, D.C.: Acropolis Books, 1991.

Simon, Seymour. *Sharks*. New York: HarperCollins, 1995.

From: Bridges to Reading, Grades K–3: Teaching Reading Skills with Children's Literature. © 1999 Suzanne I. Barchers. Teacher Ideas Press (800) 237-6124.

Generalization

Gerstein, Mordicai, and Susan Yard Harris. *Daisy's Garden.* New York: Hyperion, 1995.

Grade levels: K–1.

April has arrived, and Daisy is ready to plant her garden. All the animals gather to help her plow, dig holes, and sow the seeds. With each passing month, the garden grows while they tend it. Finally, October comes, and it's time to let the garden rest until the next spring arrives.

Activities

1. Read the book to the class. Then discuss what the weather is usually like in each month mentioned in the book. For example, April is generally variable weather. May becomes warmer with more sunshine.

2. Next, discuss what usually happens in gardens each month. Compare Daisy's garden with the gardens in your locale. Are your gardens in a drier, wetter, colder, or warmer climate?

3. Discuss the animals in Daisy's garden. Are they generally helpful or harmful? For example, people with gardens near the mountains or near forests often have trouble with deer eating the gardens. What do animals in your gardens do?

4. Check out an almanac or consult *Cracked Corn and Snow Ice Cream* (see entry under the following "Related books" section). Is the weather in the almanac generally the same as yours? Interview older relatives and friends. What do they remember from the past about trends in the weather and their effect on gardening?

5. How many seasons does this book cover? Discuss spring, summer, and fall and what gardening is like in your area from season to season. Can you garden in fewer or more seasons than those described in the book?

Related books

Fowler, Susi Greg. *Beautiful.* Illustrated by Jim Fowler. New York: Greenwillow, 1998.

Lerner, Carol. *My Backyard Garden.* New York: Morrow, 1998.

Mallet, David. *Inch by Inch: The Garden Song.* Illustrated by Ora Eitan. New York: HarperCollins, 1995.

Thomas, Elizabeth. *Green Beans.* Illustrated by Vicki Jo Redenbaugh. Minneapolis, Minn.: Carolrhoda, 1992.

Willard, Nancy. *Cracked Corn and Snow Ice Cream.* Illustrated by Jane Dyer. San Diego, Calif.: Harcourt Brace & Company, 1997.

From: Bridges to Reading, Grades K–3: Teaching Reading Skills with Children's Literature. © 1999 Suzanne I Barchers. Teacher Ideas Press (800) 237-6124.

From: Bridges to Reading, Grades K–3: Teaching Reading Skills with Children's Literature. © 1999 Suzanne I. Barchers. Teacher Ideas Press (800) 237-6124.

Lewin, Ted. *Market!* New York: Lothrop, Lee and Shepard, 1996.

Grade levels: 2–3.

People love to go to the market. Lewin takes the reader on an around-the-world tour of markets. Beginning in Ecuador, the reader then visits Nepal, Ireland, Uganda, the United States, and Morocco. The exotic places and fascinating people are beautifully portrayed through detailed, color illustrations.

Activities

1. Read about each of the markets. Discuss the features of each marketplace. Locate each on a globe or world map. Then create a simple chart, such as the example presented below, that lists each marketplace plus several categories for comparison. Have the students come up with one word for each category that encapsulates the feature of that particular marketplace.

Market	People	Food Product	Other Product
Ecuador	Colorful	Vegetables	Weavings
Nepal			
Ireland			
Uganda			
United States			
Morocco			

2. After completing the chart, have the students choose one word or phrase that describes each country. They should distinguish it from the other countries. What does the marketplace tell them about the country in general?

3. Collect as many of the books about markets from the "Related books" list below as possible. Share them and compare the markets. What can the students generalize about the countries based on the marketplaces?

Generalization

Related books

Bunting, Eve. *Market Day.* Illustrated by Holly Berry. New York: HarperCollins, 1996.

Garay, Luis. *Pedrito's Day.* New York: Orchard, 1997.

Lewin, Ted. *The Storytellers.* New York: Lothrop, Lee and Shepard, 1998.

Tchana, Katrin Hyman, and Louis Tchana Pami. *Oh, No, Toto!* Illustrated by Colin Bootman. New York: Scholastic, 1997.

Torres, Leyla. *Saturday Sancocho.* New York: Farrar, Straus & Giroux, 1995.

From: Bridges to Reading, Grades K-3: Teaching Reading Skills with Children's Literature. © 1999 Suzanne I. Barchers. Teacher Ideas Press (800) 237-6124.

From: Bridges to Reading, Grades K-3: Teaching Reading Skills with Children's Literature. © 1999 Suzanne I. Barchers. Teacher Ideas Press (800) 237-6124.

 Adler, David A. *A Picture Book of Christopher Columbus.* Illustrated by John and Alexandra Wallner. New York: Holiday House, 1991.

Grade levels: 2–3.

Born into a family of weavers in 1451, Christopher Columbus grew up in Genoa. He loved the sea, becoming a sailor. Following a pirate attack, he found himself in Portugal, where he joined his brother and ran a map shop. When Christopher wanted to sail west instead of east to the Indies, the kings of Portugal, France, and England refused to give him ships. Finally the queen of Spain gave him the three ships that he sailed to the New World.

Activities

1. Before reading this book aloud, ask the students what they know about Christopher Columbus. Do they know what his parents did or where he was born? Write down their responses on the board.

2. Define biography (a book that tell about a person's life). Read the biography aloud. Then discuss the facts about Columbus's life that the book shared.

3. Discuss the time line in the back of the book. How old was Christopher Columbus at key stages of his life, such as when his sons were born and when he landed in America?

4. Compare this book with others on the "Related books" list at the end of this section. For example, this book gives more information than Peter Sis's book but less than the book by Clint Twist. Which book do the students prefer?

5. Sample parts of Clint Twist's book to give students more information about Columbus's life. For example, read about subsequent voyages, or learn about the foods of the New World.

Related books

Anderson, Joan. *Christopher Columbus: From Vision to Voyage.* Photographs by George Ancona. New York: Dial, 1991.

Greene, Carol. *Christopher Columbus: A Great Explorer.* Chicago: Childrens Press, 1989.

Sis, Peter. *Follow the Dream.* New York: Alfred A. Knopf, 1991.

Twist, Clint. *Christopher Columbus: Discovery of the Americas.* Austin, Tex.: Raintree Steck-Vaughn, 1994.

Tunnell, Michael O. *Beauty and the Beastly Children.* Illustrated by John Emil Cymerman. New York: Morrow, 1993.

Grade levels: 2–3.

After Beauty marries Auguste, the former Beast, she discovers that his behavior is still a bit beastly. Meanwhile, Beauty gives birth to triplets who prove to be beastly as well. But once Auguste becomes involved in their care, the spell on the children is broken. The children's behavior improves, and Auguste becomes kingly once again.

Activities

1. Read the traditional story of Beauty (see the titles listed in the "Related books" section below). Then ask the students if they ever wondered what happened next in the story. Brainstorm several story scenarios.

2 Read Tunnell's story aloud. Discuss the elements of fairy tales that exist in this invented version: a king and queen, a magic spell, challenges to meet, transformation, and a happy resolution. Discuss how most fairy tales were told orally and were collected more than a hundred years ago. Contrast those with Tunnell's tale, which he created as an original story. Does this story retain the feel of a traditional fairy tale?

3. Discuss other traditional fairy tales that could have follow-up stories. What happened after Cinderella married the prince? What happened to Rumpelstiltskin? Did the Three Little Pigs continue to live happily in their brick house? What was Little Red Riding Hood like when she grew up and had children? Did Hansel and Gretel continue to have adventures together after they were reunited with their father? Create sequels to these stories, making sure that they also have a traditional feel.

Related books

Apy, Deborah. *Beauty and the Beast.* Illustrated by Michael Hague. New York: Holt, Rinehart and Winston, 1980, 1983.

Hearne, Betsy. *Beauties and Beasts.* Phoenix, Ariz.: Oryx Press, 1993.

Mayer, Marianna. *Beauty and the Beast.* Illustrated by Mercer Mayer. New York: Scholastic, 1978.

From: Bridges to Reading, Grades K–3: Teaching Reading Skills with Children's Literature. © 1999 Suzanne I. Barchers. Teacher Ideas Press (800) 237-6124.

From: Bridges to Reading, Grades K–3: Teaching Reading Skills with Children's Literature. © 1999 Suzanne I. Barchers. Teacher Ideas Press (800) 237-6124.

Climo, Shirley. *A Pride of Princesses: Princess Tales from Around the World.* Illustrated by Ruth Sanderson. New York: HarperCollins, 1999.

Grade levels: 2–3.

In a tale from China, two princesses use their sewing skills to create the Milky Way. In an Arabian tale, a princess benefits from listening to a woman's wisdom. A Tsar's son takes a frog princess as his wife. In a South African tale, a princess relies on her strength instead of her beauty. Princess Lina matures with King Thrushbeard. A tale from Guatemala and the story of Psyche complete the collection.

Activities

1. Take several days to share this rich collection of stories. Begin to analyze them by finding their various countries of origin on a globe or world map. Discuss how the different cultures contributed to the tales.

2. Create a chart that compares the elements of the tales. Use the following example as a beginning point.

Name of fairy tale	The Moon Maidens	Gulnara
Setting	Heavens	
Name of princess(es)	White Jade and Golden Bird	
Other main characters	Sky Prince, Emperor of Heavens	
Challenge	Day had become night.	
Action taken	Sisters became Sun Sisters.	
Resolution	Day returned.	

3. Adjust the elements to compare the stories while working on the chart. When finished, discuss the similarities and differences in the stories. Draw some conclusions about the features of fairy tales.

Related books

Climo, Shirley. *A Serenade of Mermaids: Mermaid Tales from Around the World.* Illustrated by Jean and Mou-sien Tseng. New York: HarperCollins, 1997.

Hearne, Betsy. *Beauties and Beasts.* Phoenix, Ariz.: Oryx Press, 1993.

Sierra, Judy, and Robert Kaminski. *Multicultural Folktales: Stories to Tell Young Children.* Phoenix, Ariz.: Oryx Press, 1991.

From: Bridges to Reading, Grades K–3: Teaching Reading Skills with Children's Literature. © 1999 Suzanne I. Barchers. Teacher Ideas Press (800) 237-6124.

Love, D. Anne. *Bess's Log Cabin Quilt.* Illustrated by Ronald Himler. New York: Holiday House, 1995.

Grade levels: 2–3.

Bess and her mother work hard as they wait for Bess's father to return from bringing settlers west on the Oregon Trail. When Bess's mother becomes ill and a bill collector informs them that Bess's father owes him $100, Bess decides to try to win a quilt contest at the fair. Bess ties for second place, winning $100, just as her father returns and tells them the debt is already paid.

Activities

1. Allow a week or two to read this book aloud. Using a map of the United States, trace the route of the Oregon Trail.

2. Create a chart that compares Bess's life with that of the students. Use the following example as a starting point, adjusting and adding to it as you read the story aloud.

Bess's Life	Students' Lives
They lived in a cabin.	Students live in houses, apartments, etc.
They made their own music.	Students listen to CDs, television, radio.
They grew their own food.	Students buy food at a grocery store.
They traveled with a wagon train and on horseback.	Students travel in cars, trains, planes.
The doctor came to the house in a buggy.	Students go to doctors, hospitals.
The father traveled.	Some parents travel for business.

3. Add a third column that demonstrates how Bess's life was like those of children today (e.g., playing, going to school).

From: Bridges to Reading, Grades K–3: Teaching Reading Skills with Children's Literature. © 1999 Suzanne I. Barchers. Teacher Ideas Press (800) 237-6124.

Genres: Historical Fiction

Related books

Johnston, Tony. *The Quilt Story.* Illustrated by Tomie dePaola. New York: Putnam, 1984.

Jonas, Ann. *The Quilt.* New York: Greenwillow, 1984.

Paul, Ann Whitford. *Eight Hands Round: A Patchwork Alphabet.* Illustrated by Jeanette Winter. New York: HarperCollins, 1991.

Willard, Nancy. *The Mountains of Quilt.* Illustrated by Tomie dePaola. San Diego, Calif.: Harcourt Brace Jovanovich, 1987.

From: Bridges to Reading, Grades K-3: Teaching Reading Skills with Children's Literature. © 1999 Suzanne I. Barchers. Teacher Ideas Press (800) 237-6124.

From: Bridges to Reading, Grades K–3: Teaching Reading Skills with Children's Literature. © 1999 Suzanne I. Barchers. Teacher Ideas Press (800) 237-6124.

Cushman, Doug. *The Mystery of King Karfu.* New York: HarperCollins, 1996.

Grade levels: 2–3.

When the Stone Chicken of King Karfu is stolen, Seymour Sleuth and his assistant and photographer, Abbott Muggs, take a ship to Egypt. The Stone Chicken holds the secret to the lost treasure, and several characters immediately prove to be suspects in the case. After interviewing the suspects and studying the clues, Seymour catches the culprit. This colorful picture book provides a lively introduction to the topic of mysteries.

Activities

1. Before reading the book, hide an item in the classroom, such as a small box with treats for each student.

2. Ask the students what they know about mysteries. Ask them how they would go about investigating a robbery in the classroom. Discuss their ideas for an investigation.

3. Begin reading the book aloud. Allow plenty of time to study the illustrations.

4. When reading aloud the list of clues, give the students time to discuss which suspect is most likely the thief. Ask the students to justify their choices. Discuss how the detective's questions led to his list of clues. Then take a vote on the three suspects. Could someone else have a motive to steal the chicken?

5. Finish reading the book. How well did the students predict the ending?

6. Tell the students that you have hidden a treasure in the classroom. They must investigate its whereabouts without physically searching for it. Tell them that they can ask you questions, but you will only respond with a *yes* or *no*. If the students have difficulty asking you appropriate questions, give them clues. When they discover the hiding place, share the treats.

Related books

Conford, Ellen. *A Case for Jenny Archer.* Illustrated by Diane Palmisciano. Boston: Little, Brown, 1988.

Laden, Nina. *Private I. Guana: The Case of the Missing Chameleon.* San Francisco: Chronicle, 1995.

Roy, Ron. *The Bald Bandit.* New York: Random House, 1997.

Saunders, Susan. *The Chilling Tale of Crescent Pond.* Illustrated by Jane Manning. New York: HarperCollins, 1998.

Roy, Ron. *The Bald Bandit.* New York: Random House, 1997.

Grade levels: 2–3.

When a detective offers Dink, Josh, and Ruth Rose a reward for finding the red-haired student who videotaped a robber leaving a bank, the children use their ingenuity to find the student. Then they discover that the detective is actually the robber, and their quick thinking leads to his capture.

Activities

1. Read the mystery aloud, allowing several days to complete this short chapter book. At the end of chapter 6, ask the students how they think the story is going to end. Record their guesses. Then ask them to list any clues that led them to their conclusions.

2. Finish reading the book. Discuss how mysteries are written, with the readers given clues to the ending throughout the book.

3. Analyze the structure of this mystery. Use the chart below to begin the analysis, filling in other clues that the students identify, along with the solution.

Title: *The Bald Bandit.*
Problem: A detective needs a videotape that shows the robber in a bank robbery.
Clue: The kids wear costumes.
Clue: The detective tells them not to look at the tape.
Clue:
Clue:
Solution:

Related books

Conford, Ellen. *A Case for Jenny Archer.* Illustrated by Diane Palmisciano. Boston: Little, Brown, 1988.

Cushman, Doug. *The Mystery of King Karfu.* New York: HarperCollins, 1996.

Laden, Nina. *Private I. Guana: The Case of the Missing Chameleon.* San Francisco: Chronicle, 1995.

Saunders, Susan. *The Chilling Tale of Crescent Pond.* Illustrated by Jane Manning. New York: HarperCollins, 1998.

From: Bridges to Reading, Grades K-3: Teaching Reading Skills with Children's Literature. © 1999 Suzanne I. Barchers. Teacher Ideas Press (800) 237-6124.

From: Bridges to Reading, Grades K–3: Teaching Reading Skills with Children's Literature. © 1999 Suzanne I. Barchers. Teacher Ideas Press (800) 237-6124.

Osborne, Mary Pope, reteller. "John Henry." In *American Tall Tales.* Illustrated by Michael McCurdy. New York: Alfred A. Knopf, 1991.

Grade levels: 2–3.

John Henry grew up to be the best steel driver in the entire country. He was working on a tunnel in the Allegheny Mountains when a salesman from the city brought a steam drill to the site. A contest was set up between John Henry and the steam drill. Although he beat the steam drill, he died in the process.

Activities

1. Read the story aloud. Discuss the use of hyperbole and how such tales of the settling of the country contributed to the work ethic in place in the United States.

2. Prepare the readers theatre version of this story, told from the point of view of John Henry's wife. The narrator plays an important role and should rehearse the script carefully. Because the parents only speak one line each, they could leave the stage after saying their lines. The machine salesman could enter the stage late in the story.

3. For props, John Henry could wear a railroad or workman's cap. A sledgehammer, fencing materials, and other tools could be propped onstage. The spoken parts are written in a casual style. The characters should sound folksy without sounding ignorant.

4. After preparing and sharing the tale, consider creating others that are inspired by tall tales.

Characters
- Narrator
- Mama
- Papa
- Polly Ann
- John Henry
- Captain Tommy
- Men
- Machine Salesman

Genres: Tall Tales

Related books

Grant, Neil. *American Folk Tales and Legends.* London: Peerage Books, 1988.

Kellogg, Steven. *Mike Fink.* New York: Morrow, 1992.

———. *Paul Bunyan.* New York: Morrow, 1984.

Schwartz, Alvin. *Whoppers: Tall Tales and Other Lies Collected from American Folklore.* New York: Harper & Row, 1975.

Wood, Audrey. *The Bunyans.* Illustrated by David Shannon. New York: Scholastic, 1996.

From: Bridges to Reading, Grades K-3: Teaching Reading Skills with Children's Literature. © 1999 Suzanne I. Barchers. Teacher Ideas Press (800) 237-6124.

Polly Ann and John Henry

Narrator: When Polly Ann arrived in this world, the moon moved in front of the sun for five full minutes. Her parents took this to mean that Polly Ann would be truly special.

Mama: You were so fine the sun winked at the world. Child, there's nothing you can't do!

Narrator: Polly Ann believed her mama. When other little girls played with their dollies, Polly Ann practiced pounding nails into wood scraps from her papa's shop. While her cousins had tea parties, Polly Ann pitched horseshoes with her papa.

Papa: My pretty Polly! How you can pound a nail and pitch a horseshoe! You make me proud!

Narrator: With all that pounding and pitching, Polly grew to be one strong young lady. Pretty, too. Fellas would come calling. But it wouldn't take long for those unsuspecting young men to decide that anyone who could pitch a game like Polly Ann would not make a good housewife. One hot day Polly was about to start a new fence down by the road. Just as she was fixing to set the gatepost, up sauntered a young man as handsome as the night and looking twice as strong.

John Henry: Looks like you could use some help, miss.

Narrator: Polly Ann looked the young man square in the eyes, hoisted her hammer, and set that post with one blow.

Polly Ann: Thanks anyway, but I rather enjoy setting posts.

John Henry: Then maybe you'd be so kind as to fetch me a dipper of water. It is mighty hot today.

Polly Ann: Help yourself. What's your name?

John Henry: My name's John Henry. And yours?

Polly Ann: Polly Ann. Where you from and where you headed?

John Henry: Yonder the next county, but now I'm off to find the new railroad. I've a hankering to pound some steel.

Polly Ann: But you've got no hammer.

John Henry: I reckon I'll just have to use yours, Miss Polly Ann.

Narrator: And that's how Polly Ann and John Henry commenced to courting. It only took two games of horseshoes to see that they were fairly matched. John Henry suggested they finish that new fence together. By the time they set the third post, they were in love. By the seventh post they were engaged. By the time the last post was pounded into place, the wedding date was set. After the wedding, John Henry was ready to move on.

From: Bridges to Reading, Grades K–3: Teaching Reading Skills with Children's Literature. © 1999 Suzanne I. Barchers. Teacher Ideas Press (800) 237-6124.

John Henry: It's time to find that railroad, Polly Ann. We'll have a fine honeymoon on our way.

Narrator: John Henry and Polly Ann headed west until they came to the Big Bend Tunnel of the Chesapeake and Ohio Railroad. Hearing the men hammering and singing as they worked made John Henry eager to join them. It didn't take long for him to find the boss.

John Henry: Captain Tommy! I would surely like to sign on as a steel-driving man!

Captain Tommy: I don't know. That's a mighty big job. You don't even have a hammer.

John Henry: I've got hers.

Men: A girl's hammer? What kind of man is he?

Narrator: Just to prove that he could do the job, Polly Ann gave over her hammer and stood in as John Henry's shaker, setting each spike in place for John Henry to hit. In no time she was calling for a bucket of water to cool down that fast-moving hammer.

Captain Tommy: You're hired! You'll get a dollar a day, a house to borrow, and your vittles. You can start right now!

Narrator: John Henry and Polly Ann settled down, happy as fleas on a dog. Before long Polly Ann and John Henry had a little one, John Henry Junior. They put every spare penny into the cookie jar for the day when they could have their own place. Then one day a man came along bragging about a newfangled machine called a steam drill.

Machine Salesman: This machine never stops! It can do the work of 20 men! Just try it out, Captain Tommy. You won't regret buying it.

Captain Tommy: I have a hard time believing your claims. But, I tell you what, how about a race between that machine and my best natural-born machine, John Henry? If John Henry wins, you give me that machine and $200. If the machine wins, I'll buy it from you.

Machine Salesman: Sounds fair enough, if your natural-born steel driver is willing!

Captain Tommy: John Henry, I'll give you $100 if you can beat that machine.

John Henry: You don't have to talk me into it. If that machine takes over, where are hardworking, natural-born folks like me going to find jobs?

Narrator: They set the day for the contest, and people from 100 miles away came to watch.

Polly Ann: John Henry, I know you feel you got to do this, but I won't be the same if anything happens to you.

John Henry: Polly, a man ain't nothing but a man. And a man's always got to do his best. I'll beat that machine, just you wait and see. That $100 can buy us our own place.

From: Bridges to Reading, Grades K–3: Teaching Reading Skills with Children's Literature. © 1999 Suzanne I. Barchers. Teacher Ideas Press (800) 237-6124.

From: Bridges to Reading, Grades K–3: Teaching Reading Skills with Children's Literature. © 1999 Suzanne I. Barchers. Teacher Ideas Press (800) 237-6124.

Narrator: The contest began. At first the steam-powered machine pulled ahead. But John Henry just grabbed a hammer in his other hand and worked harder and faster. He sang as he worked, knowing he could beat that machine. Every hour they had to call in a new shaker to keep up with all the spikes John Henry drove. The machine worked hard, too. But after eight hours, it began to shake just a little. John Henry just kept driving with both hammers, but he was getting weary, and there were no shakers left. Polly Ann pushed past the men in the tunnel and took over as the shaker.

Polly Ann: John Henry, you're going to win. You're a natural-born, steel-driving man.

Narrator: Polly kept setting those spikes as her eyes burned from the dust and smarted from the tears at watching the man she loved drive those spikes. Finally, during the ninth and last hour, the machine began to overheat. Polly Ann and John Henry just kept setting and driving.

Men: Come on, John Henry! Don't give up! You can do it!

Captain Tommy: Time's up!

Narrator: The machine wheezed and died. John Henry began to drop the hammers, but Polly Ann took both his arms with hers and brought them down together on the last two spikes. The crowd listened as that one last furious ring of the hammers echoed throughout the tunnel, and then quiet settled in the tunnel. The dust cleared and the men saw that John Henry had indeed won—by three spikes! They also saw that he lay on the ground. Polly Ann was holding him in her arms, with her tears washing the dust from his face.

John Henry: Did we win, Polly Ann?

Polly Ann: You won, John Henry. We're gonna go buy that place with our $100.

John Henry: Just give me a cool drink of water, and I'll be ready to move on, my fine Polly Ann.

Narrator: But before anyone could fetch him a drink, he had moved on forever. Polly Ann picked him up and carried him outside the tunnel and right up to their little home. A few days later, she and Junior buried John Henry on the hillside with her hammer in his hand and a steel rod across his breast. The clouds moved across the sun for five whole minutes, and the earth trembled as if a train were roaring down the tracks.

Epilogue

Polly Ann stayed on for a while, working to complete that tunnel. Some days she'd drive steel. Other days she'd be a shaker. But memories of John Henry became too much for her. She took that $100 plus all her cookie jar savings and headed west with Junior. They got that place, and every time she set a fence post with her new hammer she'd think about her natural-born, steel-driving man and tell their son how his daddy beat a newfangled machine.

©Barchers, Suzanne I. Arvada, Colo.: Storycart Press™, 1998. (www.storycart.com)
This script may be reproduced for use in a single school only.

Gwynne, Fred. *The King Who Rained.* New York: Simon & Schuster, 1970.

Grade levels: 2–3.

In this amusing book, a king rains, forks lay in the road, a mole perches on the daddy's nose, lambs gamble, the mommy has a frog in her throat, and sometimes mommy uses throat spray when she's horse. The use of illustrations to show the literal quality of idioms makes this book ideal for introducing the concept of idiomatic language.

Activities

1. Show the cover of the book. Ask the students why it is humorous. Discuss how the words *reign* and *rain* can be confused because of their identical sound.

2. Share the book, discussing how some sayings may have originated. For example, giving the house two coats of paint may have a direct link to putting on a coat (garment).

3. Begin to collect examples of idiomatic language as they show up in books or spoken language. Have the students create their own books of idiomatic language, using this one as a model.

4. If any students in the class speak another language, ask them if they have idioms in their language. Ask them to share any that they know, explaining the background if possible. Students can also interview their parents or grandparents to learn of other examples.

5. Consult Marvin Terban's *Mad As a Wet Hen and Other Funny Idioms* or James Cox's *Put Your Foot in Your Mouth and Other Silly Sayings* (see the "Related books" section on page 37) for explanations behind common idioms. Give the students examples and have them create illustrations to go with them. For example, a cartoonist once showed a dog with its head laying nearby. The owner, just entering the house, said something like, "Well, you finally did it. You barked your fool head off." Discuss the humor that results from such use of idiomatic language.

From: Bridges to Reading, Grades K–3: Teaching Reading Skills with Children's Literature. © 1999 Suzanne I. Barchers. Teacher Ideas Press (800) 237-6124.

Related books

Cox, James A. *Put Your Foot in Your Mouth and Other Silly Sayings.* Illustrated by Sam Q. Weissman. New York: Random House, 1980.

Grover, Max. *Max's Wacky Taxi Day.* San Diego, Calif.: Harcourt Brace & Company, 1997.

Gwynne, Fred. *A Chocolate Moose for Dinner.* New York: Simon & Schuster, 1976.

Klasky, Charles. *Rugs Have Naps (But Never Take Them).* Illustrated by Mike Venezia. Chicago: Childrens Press, 1984.

Terban, Marvin. *Mad As a Wet Hen and Other Funny Idioms.* Illustrated by Giulio Maestro. New York: Clarion, 1987.

———. *Punching the Clock: Funny Action Idioms.* Illustrated by Tom Huffman. New York: Clarion, 1990.

———. *Scholastic Dictionary of Idioms: More Than 600 Phrases, Sayings and Expressions.* New York: Scholastic, 1996.

From: Bridges to Reading, Grades K-3: Teaching Reading Skills with Children's Literature. © 1999 Suzanne I. Barchers. Teacher Ideas Press (800) 237-6124.

Raffi, and Debi Pike. *Like Me and You.* Illustrated by Lillian Hoban. New York: Crown, 1985, 1994.

Grade levels: 2–3.

The children in this book live all over the world: England, France, Canada, Egypt, Israel, Australia, China, Russia, India, Germany, Spain. Each child is depicted mailing, reading, or receiving a letter. The brief text emphasizes that all the children are alike. A song is included in the book.

Activities

1. Read the book aloud. Discuss what the children are doing with the mail.

2. Read the book again. This time have the students find each of the countries on a large map. Place a sticky note on each country with the country's name in large letters.

3. Discuss the format of a friendly letter. Have the students choose a relative, sibling, friend, or neighbor to write to. If it is near Valentine's Day, consider having the students write a love letter. If it is after the winter holidays, consider assigning a thank-you letter.

4. Have the students write letters and bring in postage to mail them.

5. Set up a letter writing center where students can regularly use paper and envelopes to mail letters. Consider a field trip to the post office to learn how mail is organized, transported, and delivered. Compare U.S. mail service with e-mail.

6. Because the illustrator's style is for all the children's faces to look strikingly similar, compare this book with *People* by Peter Spier (see the following "Related books" section). Discuss how Spier's book focuses on cultural differences in looks, features, dress, and housing.

Related books

Cobb, Nancy. *Letter Writer Book.* Illustrated by Laura Cornell. Pleasantville, N.Y.: Reader's Digest Kids, 1994.

Leedy, Loreen. *Messages in the Mailbox: How to Write a Letter.* New York: Holiday House, 1991.

Spier, Peter. *People.* New York: Doubleday, 1980.

Williams, Vera B. *Stringbean's Trip to the Shining Sea.* Illustrated by Jennifer Williams. New York: Greenwillow, 1988.

From: Bridges to Reading, Grades K–3: Teaching Reading Skills with Children's Literature. © 1999 Suzanne I. Barchers. Teacher Ideas Press (800) 237-6124.

From: Bridges to Reading, Grades K–3: Teaching Reading Skills with Children's Literature. © 1999 Suzanne I. Barchers. Teacher Ideas Press (800) 237-6124.

Ada, Alma Flor. *Dear Peter Rabbit.* Illustrated by Leslie Tryon. New York: Atheneum, 1994.

Grade levels: 2–3.

Pig One invites Peter Rabbit to his housewarming party, but Peter Rabbit is in bed with a cold. But, as luck would have it, a disaster with a wolf forces the cancellation and rescheduling of the party. Goldilocks and Baby Bear become friends, and Goldilocks also becomes acquainted with Little Red Riding Hood. Finally, the pigs hold their housewarming party, complete with wolf tail soup.

Activities

1. Read the story aloud to the students, discussing the stories that the letters represent. Discuss why the characters might want to write to one another.

2. Read a variety of other fairy or folk tales, using collections or individually illustrated stories. If possible, read Janet and Allan Ahlberg's *The Jolly Postman or Other People's Letters* (see the "Related books" section below).

3. Brainstorm letters that the students could write between characters. For example, perhaps Cinderella could write to her sisters, asking them to come to a ball where they might meet their own princes.

4. Create one or two letters as a class. Discuss the correct form for the letter, showing how the letter should begin and end. Discuss the differences based on whether the letter is a business letter or a friendly letter, using examples from *Dear Peter Rabbit.*

5. Have the students create their own letters. Share them as a class.

Related books

Ahlberg, Janet, and Allan Ahlberg. *The Jolly Christmas Postman.* Boston: Little, Brown, 1991.

———. *The Jolly Postman or Other People's Letters.* Boston: Little, Brown, 1986.

Cobb, Nancy. *Letter Writer Book.* Illustrated by Laura Cornell. Pleasantville, N.Y.: Reader's Digest Kids, 1994.

Leedy, Loreen. *Messages in the Mailbox: How to Write a Letter.* New York: Holiday House, 1991.

Jonas, Ann. *Color Dance.* New York: Trumpet, 1989.

Grade levels: K–1.

In this simple book, youngsters dance with scarves of various colors. They present the scarves singly and then in pairs, showing what colors result when they are mixed. The illustrations also demonstrate the effect of mixing several colors or adding white or gray.

Activities

1. Read the book aloud. Show the color wheel at the end of the book. Ask the students why they think the author wrote and illustrated this book. Discuss how authors often get ideas by noticing what kinds of books are needed and then creating books to fill the need.

2. Collect a variety of informational books on any topic. Review the books briefly. Ask the students to identify why the author wrote each of the books.

3. Collect scarves in the primary colors (red, yellow, and blue) and experiment with replicating effects described in the book. Note the caution regarding color choices at the end of the book.

4. Use watercolors to replicate the mixing of the colors as demonstrated in the book. Let the students experiment with adding white and gray.

5. Brainstorm other ways that the author could have taught colors. Perhaps she could have made a book about mixing paints, using dyes, or layering tissue paper. Have the students work in small groups to create their own color books. Share the books with other classes or place them in the library for student use.

Related books

McMillan, Bruce. *Growing Colors.* New York: Morrow, 1988.

Otto, Carolyn. *What Color Is Camouflage?* Illustrated by Megan Lloyd. New York: HarperCollins, 1996.

Schroeder, Pamela J. P., and Jean M. Donisch. *What's the Big Idea? Colors.* Vero Beach, Fla.: Rourke, 1996.

Walsh, Ellen Stoll. *Mouse Paint.* New York: Trumpet, 1989.

From: Bridges to Reading, Grades K–3: Teaching Reading Skills with Children's Literature. © 1999 Suzanne I. Barchers. Teacher Ideas Press (800) 237-6124.

From: Bridges to Reading, Grades K–3: Teaching Reading Skills with Children's Literature. © 1999 Suzanne I. Barchers. Teacher Ideas Press (800) 237-6124.

Murphy, Stuart J. *Too Many Kangaroo Things to Do!* Illustrated by Kevin O'Malley. New York: HarperCollins, 1996.

Grade levels: 2–3.

It's Kangaroo's birthday, and he tries to find someone to play with. Each animal tells Kangaroo he is too busy to play. For example, the emu has to bake one cake, and spread two colors of frosting. As Kangaroo visits his friends, the tasks multiply. Finally, the friends hold a surprise party for him, having had a total of 100 kangaroo things to do.

Activities

1. Read the book aloud. Periodically pause to allow the students to discuss the number of activities each animal has to do.

2. Make a list of things the students do during the day and multiply them as in the story. For example, if 25 students use four books during the day, 100 books get used.

3. Look around the room. How many tables are there? Multiply the number of tables times their four legs. Find other items to multiply and compile the information.

4. Discuss why the author wrote this book. Did it help the students understand multiplication? Do they know other books that helped them understand math concepts? Discuss those books or share some from the "Related books" list below.

5. Have the students use this book as a model to create their own multiplication story. Perhaps they could feature children preparing for Halloween or animals preparing for a wedding celebration.

Related books

Anno, Masaichiro, and Mitsumasa Anno. *Anno's Mysterious Multiplying Jar.* New York: Philomel, 1983.

Giganti, Paul. *Each Orange Had 8 Slices: A Counting Book.* Illustrated by Donald Crews. New York: Trumpet, 1992.

Hulme, Joy N. *Counting by Kangaroos.* Illustrated by Betsy Scheld. New York: W. H. Freeman, 1995.

Baron, Alan. *Red Fox Dances.* Cambridge, Mass.: Candlewick Press, 1996.

Grade levels: K–1.

Red Fox is very hungry as he prowls through the woods looking for dinner. When he sees Little Pig and other animals dancing, he decides to show them how to dance. He joins them and becomes so engrossed in his antics that he doesn't notice his potential dinners disappearing into the woods.

Activities

1. Read this short book aloud. Take time to allow students to predict the events as you read the book.

2. List the names of the characters on the board, beginning with Red Fox. Discuss their characteristics, emphasizing that the reader knows the most about Red Fox.

3. Distribute copies of the characteristics box template on page 43 and tagboard. Have the students write the name *Red Fox* on one side of the cube. Then have them write a characteristic on each side of the cube. Glue the box template to a piece of tagboard. Then have the students cut out the box and fold it along the dotted lines to make a box. (The box can be used for storage of small items.)

4. For a variation, have the students write a different character's name on each cube, adding a characteristic under the name.

5. To reinforce verbs, have the students write one action word describing Red Fox's actions on each side of the cube. For example, he danced, skipped, jumped, kicked, bounced, and rocked and rolled. Roll one of the finished cubes. Have the students perform the activity that displays on the top side of the cube.

Related books

Baron, Alan. *Little Pig's Bouncy Ball.* Cambridge, Mass.: Candlewick Press, 1996.

Hayes, Sarah. *Nine Ducks Nine.* Cambridge, Mass.: Candlewick Press, 1990.

Hendra, Sue. *Oliver's Wood.* Cambridge, Mass.: Candlewick Press, 1996.

Hutchins, Pat. *Little Pink Pig.* New York: Greenwillow, 1994.

From: Bridges to Reading, Grades K–3: Teaching Reading Skills with Children's Literature. © 1999 Suzanne I. Barchers. Teacher Ideas Press (800) 237-6124.

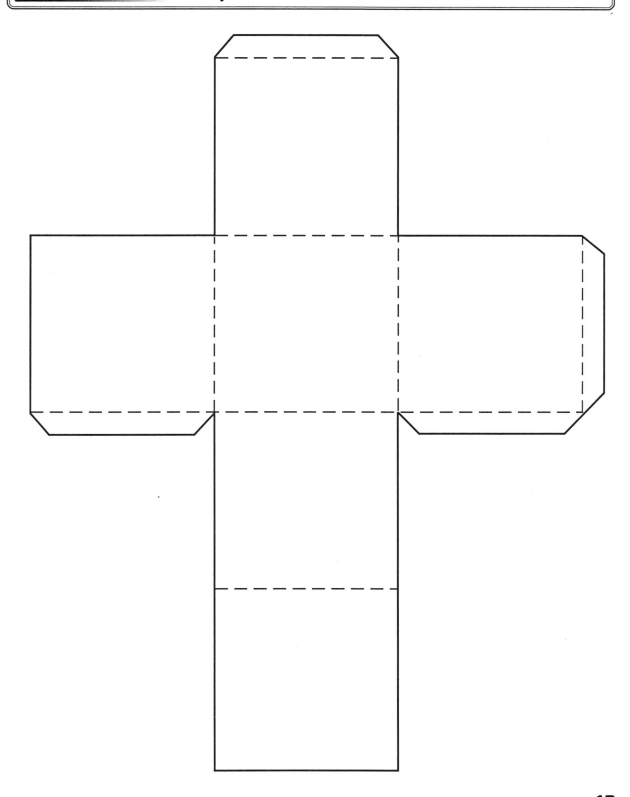

From: Bridges to Reading, Grades K–3: Teaching Reading Skills with Children's Literature. © 1999 Suzanne I. Barchers. Teacher Ideas Press (800) 237-6124.

Literary Elements and Features: Characterization

 Ehrlich, Amy. *Cinderella.* Illustrated by Susan Jeffers. New York: Dial, 1985. Grade levels: 2–3.

In this classic retelling, lavishly illustrated, Cinderella yearns to go to the ball. Her godmother turns a pumpkin into a coach, six mice into horses, a rat into a coachman, and six lizards into footmen. She also gives Cinderella a beautiful gown. Cinderella goes to the ball, where she entrances the prince. Finally, she wears the glass slipper and marries the prince.

Activities

1. Read the story aloud, taking time to enjoy the illustrations. Then explain that the students are going to create a résumé, a record of background and skills, for Cinderella. Create a form similar to the example below.

Character's Name
Address
Education and Training
Work History
Skills
Goals

2. Create similar résumés for the stepsisters.

3. Expand on what the students know about Cinderella by developing her character more fully. Decide as a group or individually what Cinderella would have as her favorite food, color, flower, wild animal, pet, game, hobby, bedtime story, beverage, snack, vacation spot, book, magazine, movie, music, item of clothing, relative, and toy from childhood.

4. Compare this version with other versions of *Cinderella*. Judy Sierra's book (see the "Related books" section below) contains several variations on the story. Also consult other titles listed below or the library.

Related books

Climo, Shirley. *The Egyptian Cinderella.* Illustrated by Ruth Heller. New York: HarperCollins, 1989.

———. *The Irish Cinderlad.* Illustrated by Loretta Krupinski. New York: HarperCollins, 1996.

———. *The Korean Cinderella.* Illustrated by Ruth Heller. New York: HarperCollins, 1993.

Martin, Rafe. *The Rough-Face Girl.* Illustrated by David Shannon. New York: G. P. Putnam's Sons, 1992.

Sierra, Judy. *Cinderella.* Phoenix, Ariz.: Oryx Press, 1992.

From: Bridges to Reading: Grades K–3: Teaching Reading Skills with Children's Literature. © 1999 Suzanne I. Barchers. Teacher Ideas Press (800) 237-6124.

Hoff, Syd. *Happy Birthday, Danny and the Dinosaur!* New York: HarperCollins, 1995.

Grade levels: K–1.

Danny invites his friend, the dinosaur, to his birthday party. Because the dinosaur is a hundred million years and one day old, they celebrate his birthday, too. They all decorate, sing, play "Pin the Tail on the Donkey," and have ice cream and cake. Both Danny and the dinosaur conclude that this was the best birthday party they ever had.

Activities

1. Begin reading the story. After displaying the first page, ask the students where they think Danny is, based on the picture and the sign. When Danny invites the dinosaur to his party, as shown on the next page spread, ask the students what they can conclude about where the dinosaur probably lives.

2. When reading the part about how the dinosaur helps with the decorating, ask the students what the dinosaur's behavior with the children riding his back tells them about his disposition.

3. When the children sang a song, the others clapped. When the dinosaur sang, everyone covered their ears. What can the children conclude about the dinosaur's singing ability?

4. Ask the students why they think the dinosaur had to have so much ice cream.

5. After showing Danny and the dinosaur blowing out the candles, ask the students how they think the story will end. Read the last page. What other endings would work well with the story? What do the students think might happen next? Will Danny take the dinosaur back to the museum? Will they go outside to play? Discuss the possibilities and accept all reasonable answers.

Related books

Bunting, Eve. *Happy Birthday, Dear Duck.* Illustrated by Jan Brett. New York: Clarion, 1988.

Murphy, Stuart J. *Too Many Kangaroo Things to Do.* Illustrated by Kevin O'Malley. New York: HarperCollins, 1996.

Spirn, Michele Sobel. *A Know-Nothing Birthday.* Illustrated by R. W. Alley. New York: HarperCollins, 1997.

From: Bridges to Reading, Grades K–3: Teaching Reading Skills with Children's Literature. © 1999 Suzanne I. Barchers. Teacher Ideas Press (800) 237-6124.

Calmenson, Stephanie. *The Children's Aesop.* Illustrated by Robert Byrd. Honesdale, Penn.: Boyds Mills Press, 1992.

Grade levels: 2–3.

In this book, 28 fables are retold and illustrated. Familiar tales, such as "The Hare and the Tortoise" and "The Dog and His Bone," are included, along with less commonly known tales, such as "The Ant and the Dove" and "The Bundle of Sticks."

Activities

1. Begin by reading a familiar tale, such as "The Hare and the Tortoise." Do not read the moral at the end. Instead, ask the students what conclusion or lesson the fable illustrates. Accept any reasonable answer.

2. Read other familiar tales that will prompt easy conclusions. Discuss the morals as prompted by the fables.

3. Choose a moral but do not read that fable aloud. For example, choose the moral *Look before you leap* from "The Fox and the Goat." Tell the students the moral. Then ask them what they think the moral means. Next, ask them to brainstorm story ideas that would lead to the moral or conclusion. Write the ideas on the board. Then work with the class to create a fable that illustrates the moral.

4. Divide the class into groups of four or five students. Give each group a moral from which they are to create a story. Consider the following morals:

   When you try to be something you're not, you end up being nothing at all.
   Kindness works better than force.
   Never trust a gossip.
   A friend who leaves you in time of need is no friend at all.
   You can't judge a book by its cover.
   Slotted spoons don't hold much soup.

Related books

Carle, Eric. *Twelve Tales From Aesop.* New York: Philomel, 1980.

Galdone, Paul. *Three Aesop Fox Fables.* New York: Clarion, 1971.

Heins, Ethel. *The Cat and the Cook and Other Fables of Krylov.* Illustrated by Anita Lobel. New York: Greenwillow, 1995.

From: Bridges to Reading, Grades K-3: Teaching Reading Skills with Children's Literature. © 1999 Suzanne I. Barchers. Teacher Ideas Press (800) 237-6124.

Weeks, Sarah. *Mrs. McNosh Hangs Up Her Wash.* Illustrated by Nadine Bernard Westcott. New York: HarperCollins, 1998.

Grade levels: K–1.

Every Monday Mrs. McNosh washes her clothes in a big barrel and hangs them up to dry on a clothesline. In humorous rhyme, the reader discovers that she hangs up all sorts of things in addition to her clothes: the newspaper, the dog, his dish and bone, and even the phone. Students will love this silly, easy-to-read story.

Activities

1. Before reading the story, use sticky notes to cover the last word on each page. Begin to read the story aloud, pausing before the last word in each rhyme. Ask the students to predict the word that you have concealed.

2. Once students have learned that there is a rhyming pattern, they will be able to predict the words more accurately. However, because the text is occasionally fanciful, encourage the students to read the illustrations also.

3. Make a list of all the items Mrs. McNosh hung up on her line. Then brainstorm other rhyming pairs of words that could be used to make additional verses. Encourage the students to write a version of what Mrs. McNosh hung up on the clothesline the next Monday.

4. Create a new version of a Mrs. McNosh story. Consider *Mrs. McNosh Cleans Up Her House* as a theme. Other ideas include taking a walk, playing with her pet, riding on the bus, going to work, and taking a trip.

Related books

Karlin, Nurit. *The Fat Cat Sat on the Mat.* New York: HarperCollins, 1996.

Marshall, James. *Fox on the Job.* New York: Trumpet, 1988.

Oppenheim, Joanne. *"Not Now!" Said the Cow.* Illustrated by Chris Demarest. New York: Bantam Books, 1989.

Smith, Janice Lee. *Wizard and Wart in Trouble.* New York: HarperCollins, 1998.

From: Bridges to Reading, Grades K–3: Teaching Reading Skills with Children's Literature. © 1999 Suzanne I. Barchers. Teacher Ideas Press (800) 237-6124.

Stevenson, James. *Popcorn.* New York: Greenwillow, 1998.

Grade levels: 2–3.

This collection of poetry depicts a variety of poetry styles. Some poems, such as "Henry's Farm," are humorous. Others, such as "Under the Hill," are quiet observations. Imagery is strong in "May Morning," and students will appreciate the poignancy in "Gentle Dog."

Activities

1. Prepare the poem "Driftwood" by copying it onto an overhead transparency. Use sticky notes to cover up the third line. Read the poem aloud, skipping the third line. After reading the poem, return to the third line and ask the students what else might be scattered along the beach. Encourage them to study the illustration as they make their predictions. Remove the sticky notes and identify the words Stevenson used.

2. Copy "Romeo" onto an overhead transparency. Cover the picture of the skunk and the last word, *tuxedo.* Read the poem aloud and ask the students what they think the skunk looked like he was wearing. Accept all reasonable answers. Then show the picture of the skunk. What do they predict now? Then show the last word. Discuss how they could have used the picture to guess the word *tuxedo,* reading it even if they had never seen it before.

3. Copy "The Dredge," onto an overhead transparency. Cover the last word with a sticky note. Read the poem aloud, discussing the use of rhyme throughout. Can the students predict the last word? If they don't predict it, tell them that it doesn't have to be a common word. Show them what Stevenson wrote and discuss how he used a made-up word to fit his poem.

Related books

Cassedy, Sylvia. *Zoomrimes: Poems About Things That Go.* Illustrated by Michele Chessare. New York: HarperCollins, 1993.

Esbensen, Barbara Juster. *Echoes for the Eye: Poems to Celebrate Patterns in Nature.* Illustrated by Helen K. Davie. New York: HarperCollins, 1996.

Hopkins, Lee Bennett. *Good Rhymes, Good Times.* Illustrated by Frané Lessac. New York: HarperCollins, 1995.

Kuskin, Karla. *The Sky Is Always in the Sky.* Illustrated by Isabelle Dervaux. New York: HarperCollins, 1998.

Steig, Jeanne. *Alpha Beta Chowder.* Illustrated by William Steig. New York: HarperCollins, 1992.

From: Bridges to Reading, Grades K–3: Teaching Reading Skills with Children's Literature. © 1999 Suzanne I. Barchers. Teacher Ideas Press (800) 237-6124.

From: Bridges to Reading, Grades K–3: Teaching Reading Skills with Children's Literature. © 1999 Suzanne I. Barchers. Teacher Ideas Press (800) 237-6124.

Literary Elements and Features: Fact

Timmel, Carol Ann. *Tabitha: The Fabulous Flying Feline.* Illustrated by Laura Kelly. New York: Walker, 1996.

Grade levels: K–1.

Carol Ann's cat traveled from New York to Los Angeles in the luggage compartment of an airplane. But when they arrived, Tabitha is missing. The plane returns to New York with Tabitha, who had escaped from her carrier during the flight. For 13 days she flew across the country while searches continued in-between flights. Finally, bowing to pressure from the media, the airline grounded the plane long enough for Carol Ann to coax Tabitha out of her hiding place.

Activities

1. Read the story aloud to the students, but before reading the follow-up note on the last page, ask them if they think the story is true. Reread the story, discussing the features that make it seem pretend (such as the often amusing illustrations) and those that indicate it might be true. Then read the last page.

2. Ask the students how the writer knew some of the details, such as the fact that the cat licked water from the pipes or peeked through a trapdoor. Did the writer assume some of these details to make the story more interesting? Make a list of the details that the author surmised.

3. Ask the students if they have ever lost a pet. What did they do? Did they find it? How long was it lost? Would their experience make as unbelievable a story as this one? Discuss how authors often use their own experiences when they write.

4. Arrange to visit an airport and board a plane. Interview the guide about how pets are transported. If you can't visit an airport or board a plane, call an airline and ask about the restrictions for pet travel. Many airlines allow one or two small pets per flight to travel with the passengers in the main cabin.

Related books

Jackson, Carolyn. *The Flying Ark.* Illustrated by Graham Bardell. New York: W. H. Freeman, 1990.

McGeorge, Constance W. *Boomer's Big Day.* Illustrated by Mary Whyte. San Francisco: Chronicle, 1994.

Tunnell, Michael O. *Mailing May.* Illustrated by Ted Rand. New York: Greenwillow, 1997.

Literary Elements and Features: Fact

Jackson, Carolyn. *The Flying Ark.* Illustrated by Graham Bardell. New York: W. H. Freeman, 1990.

Grade levels: 2–3.

When exotic animals must be transported, they often fly. However, they may have individual needs that must be met. For example, gorillas are nervous fliers who spend a lot of time trying to get out of their cages. Dolphins fly in a canvas hammock and receive a continuous shower and massage during the flight. Learn how a variety of animals travel in this fascinating picture book.

Activities

1. Ask the students if they have ever flown in a plane. How do they feel on long flights? For those who haven't flown, compare long flights to long car rides. Read the introduction of the book to the students. Then read about the flying requirements and experiences for several animals. You will probably need to share the book during several periods.

2. Travel agents gather a variety of facts about their customers, creating a profile of their needs when flying. For example, some travelers prefer window seats while others prefer aisle seats. Some travelers have special diets. Keeping these facts on record helps the travel agent plan a better trip. Create flying profiles for each of the animals in the book. Consider including the information on page 51.

Related books

McGeorge, Constance W. *Boomer's Big Day.* Illustrated by Mary Whyte. San Francisco: Chronicle, 1994.

Timmel, Carol Ann. *Tabitha: The Fabulous Flying Feline.* Illustrated by Laura Kelly. New York: Walker, 1996.

Tunnell, Michael O. *Mailing May.* Illustrated by Ted Rand. New York: Greenwillow, 1997.

From: Bridges to Reading, Grades K–3: Teaching Reading Skills with Children's Literature. © 1999 Suzanne I. Barchers. Teacher Ideas Press (800) 237-6124.

ANIMAL PASSENGER PROFILE

Name of animal: _____

Container: _____

Companion needs: _____

_____

Dietary needs: _____

_____

Treats: _____

_____

Special needs: _____

_____

Temperament: _____

_____

Other information: _____

_____

From: Bridges to Reading, Grades K–3: Teaching Reading Skills with Children's Literature. © 1999 Suzanne I. Barchers. Teacher Ideas Press (800) 237-6124.

Martin, Linda. *When Dinosaurs Go Visiting.* San Francisco: Chronicle, 1993.

Grade levels: K–1.

Before dinosaurs go visiting, they get ready just like humans: They groom themselves, put on clean clothes, and prepare gifts and food. When they arrive, they visit, chat, eat a fine meal, clean up, dance, and have a great time. When it is time to go home, they hug and kiss everyone good-bye. The endpapers show photographs of their visit.

Activities

1. Before reading the book aloud, ask the students to list all the things they do before they go to visit friends or relatives. Write their contributions on the board. Create a short paragraph about a visit you recently made and write it on the board for the students to read.

2. Tell the students that you are going to read aloud a book about dinosaurs who visit their friends. Read the book through, allowing time to enjoy the illustrations.

3. Review the book and ask the students to list all the things the dinosaurs did that are similar to things they do before, during, and after a visit. List these activities on the board.

4. Next, ask the students to decide what dinosaurs could probably really do. Introduce the word *fiction*. Explain to the students that the paragraph you wrote about your visit is factual because it is based on something that really happened. Similarly, any paragraphs that they would write about their visits would be factual. Contrast that with the book, which is based on a fanciful idea that involves giving dinosaurs human behaviors. Ask the students if they can think of other books that are fiction. Discuss why those are fiction, rather than informational books. (Introducing the word *nonfiction* may be confusing at this point.)

Related books

Griffith, Helen V. *Dinosaur Habitat.* Illustrated by Sonja Lamut. New York: Greenwillow, 1998.

Hoff, Syd. *Happy Birthday, Danny and the Dinosaur!* New York: HarperCollins, 1995.

Prelutsky, Jack. *Tyrannosaurus Was a Beast.* Illustrated by Arnold Lobel. New York: Greenwillow, 1998.

Yorinks, Arthur. *Ugh.* Illustrated by Richard Egielski. New York: Farrar, Straus & Giroux, 1990.

From: Bridges to Reading, Grades K–3: Teaching Reading Skills with Children's Literature. © 1999 Suzanne I. Barchers. Teacher Ideas Press (800) 237-6124.

From: Bridges to Reading, Grades K–3: Teaching Reading Skills with Children's Literature. © 1999 Suzanne I. Barchers. Teacher Ideas Press (800) 237-6124.

Perlman, Janet. *The Emperor Penguin's New Clothes.* New York: Scholastic, 1994.

Grade levels: 2–3.

In this variant on Hans Christian Andersen's story of the vain emperor, a penguin suffers for his pride. Devoted to clothes and fashion, the Emperor Penguin proves to be easy prey for the two scoundrels who claim they are weaving wonderful cloth. During the parade, a young penguin points out that the Emperor is wearing no clothes, but in spite of his red beak, he marches on bravely.

Activities

1. Before reading the story, ask the students if they have ever wanted something to be true when they knew deep down inside that it wasn't. Introduce the story, explaining that someone discovers just how foolish he can be.

2. Read the story aloud. Take time to discuss and appreciate some of the rich vocabulary: *scoundrels, sensational, simpleton, exquisite.* Also point out several examples of interesting compound words: *trainbearers, workmanship,* and *simpleminded.*

3. Some students may already be familiar with the traditional story. Ask the students if this story could really happen. Do penguins wear clothing? Do they have an emperor? Discuss how penguins almost look like they are wearing tuxedos. Is this perhaps why the author decided to use penguins for her version? Discuss how this story is fiction because it was made up by the author and contains elements that could not possibly occur.

4. Read a traditional version of *The Emperor's New Clothes* (see the "Related books" section below). Ask the students to consider if the traditional version could really happen. Explain that Hans Christian Andersen wrote the story to teach a lesson, but that it is fiction also. What lesson can the students learn from this story?

Related books

Bell, Anthea. *The Emperor's New Clothes.* Illustrated by Dorothée Duntze. New York: Henry Holt, 1986.

Levinson, Riki. *The Emperor's New Clothes.* Illustrated by Robert Byrd. New York: Dutton, 1991.

Stevens, Janet. *The Emperor's New Clothes.* New York: Holiday House, 1985.

Kraus, Robert. *Little Louis and the Baby Bloomer.* Illustrated by Jose Aruego and Ariane Dewey. New York: HarperCollins, 1998.

Grade levels: K–1.

Summary: Little Louie couldn't do much of anything. His brother, Leo, tried to teach him how to pull a wagon and throw a ball, but Little Louie wouldn't even talk. Leo persists in trying to help him, even though his parents insist Little Louie is simply a late bloomer. Finally, Little Louie blooms into a competent little lion.

Activities

1. Ask the students if they have younger brothers or sisters. Do they remember when they learned to talk, walk, or throw a ball? If they don't have siblings, do they remember when they themselves started to walk and talk? Do any of them try to help their siblings or other youngsters? Do they ever get frustrated when trying to help?

2. Read the story aloud. Talk about how Leo continues to try to teach Little Louie even though Little Louie can't seem to do anything right. Ask the students what the message of this story is. Possible answers include: that you can't give up; that children learn things at their own rate; that you can help others learn things.

3. Ask the students what lesson this book teaches them that they can use in the classroom. Are they all learning to read at the same time? Can some of them throw a ball better than others?

4. Create an illustration of Leo on a bulletin board. List the things that Leo did, such as teaching his brother how to throw a ball. Tell the students that you would like them to be a "Leo" at least once a day by helping another student. Post examples of "Leos" on the bulletin board as students help teach others.

Related books

Blume, Judy. *The Pain and the Great One.* Illustrated by Irene Trivas. Scarsdale, N.Y.: Bradbury Press, 1974.

Waddell, Martin. *John Joe and the Big Hen.* Illustrated by Paul Howard. Cambridge, Mass.: Candlewick Press, 1995.

———. *Once There Were Giants.* Illustrated by Penny Dale. Cambridge, Mass.: Candlewick Press, 1989.

From: Bridges to Reading, Grades K–3: Teaching Reading Skills with Children's Literature. © 1999 Suzanne I. Barchers. Teacher Ideas Press (800) 237-6124.

From: Bridges to Reading, Grades K–3: Teaching Reading Skills with Children's Literature. © 1999 Suzanne I. Barchers. Teacher Ideas Press (800) 237-6124.

Shannon, George. *Heart to Heart.* Illustrated by Steve Björkman. Boston: Houghton Mifflin, 1995.

Grade levels: 2–3.

Squirrel receives a valentine from Mole telling him that he is coming over with a cake to share. In desperation, Squirrel tries to create an elaborate valentine so Mole won't realize he has forgotten this special day. Finally, he collects souvenirs from their various adventures and creates a memento of all their good times together.

Activities

1. This book deserves to be shared at any time of the year. Ask the students if they have ever forgotten a special event, such as someone's birthday. Read the story aloud, but don't share the title. Discuss what Squirrel discovered—that a valentine doesn't have to be fancy but that it does need to have "heart" behind it. Ask the students what they learned from the story. Have they ever given handmade gifts that were special because of the memories they represented or the effort involved in making?

2. Ask the students what title they would give the story. Then share George Shannon's choice of title. Do they think it captures the main idea of the story?

3. Create a card writing center, called the "Heart to Heart Writing Center." Stock it with construction paper, markers, crayons, stickers, stars, and other supplies. Post a calendar that notes the students' birthdays, Mother's Day, Father's Day, birthdays of various staff members, and other important days. Encourage the students to use the writing center to create birthday cards, get well cards, encouragement cards, and other cards.

Related books

Brown, Marc. *Arthur's Valentine.* Boston: Little, Brown, 1980.

Hoban, Lillian. *Silly Tilly's Valentine.* New York: HarperCollins, 1998.

Model, Frank. *One Zillion Valentines.* New York: Trumpet, 1981.

Prelutsky, Jack. *It's Valentine's Day.* Illustrated by Yossi Abolafia. New York: Greenwillow, 1983.

Numeroff, Laura. *If You Give a Pig a Pancake.* Illustrated by Felicia Bond. New York: HarperCollins, 1998.

Grade levels: K–1.

A pig comes to visit, and the little girl gives it a pancake. Of course, the pig wants syrup, gets sticky, and consequently needs a bath. This leads to making bubbles and finding a rubber duck, which reminds the pig of the farm. Each event sets in motion another event, leading the story right back to the beginning.

Activities

1. The events in this story drive the narrative order, with each request by the pig triggering the next event. Read the story aloud. Once the students recognize the triggers, ask them to predict what the pig will want next.

2. Create a map of the narrative. Begin in the kitchen of the house and move through the story, writing the places and events on the board. Draw a map or use a chart such as that in the example below.

3. Create a spin-off from the story. Brainstorm possible scenarios, such as giving a fox some French fries, giving a kitten some catnip, or giving an elephant an egg. Use a narrative map to plan the events and triggers. Then write the story, using the same circular process so that the story returns to the beginning.

Location	Event	Trigger
Kitchen	Pig eats a pancake.	Pig gets sticky.
Bathroom	Pig needs bubbles and duck.	Duck reminds pig of farm.
Bedroom	Looking for a suitcase.	Pig finds tap shoes.

56

From: Bridges to Reading: Teaching Reading Skills with Children's Literature, Grades K-3. © 1999 Suzanne I. Barchers. Teacher Ideas Press (800) 237-6124.

Related books

Hutchins, Pat. *Rosie's Walk.* New York: Macmillan, 1968.

Numeroff, Laura. *If You Give a Moose a Muffin.* Illustrated by Felicia Bond. New York: HarperCollins, 1991.

———. *If You Give a Mouse a Cookie.* Illustrated by Felicia Bond. New York: Harper, 1985.

From: Bridges to Reading, Grades K-3: Teaching Reading Skills with Children's Literature. © 1999 Suzanne I. Barchers. Teacher Ideas Press (800) 237-6124.

Schwartz, Amy. *A Teeny Tiny Baby.* New York: Orchard, 1994.

Grade levels: 2–3.

Life changes when a baby arrives. With seemingly little effort a baby can get anything he or she wants. Told from the point of view of the baby, the narrator takes readers through a set of experiences in a variety of settings. Children will enjoy recalling their experiences as babies, and adults will appreciate the humor.

Activities

1. Read through the story. Discuss all the places the baby goes in the course of a day. Then discuss all the places the baby might go in a week.

2. The story holds together through its description of all the places the baby goes. Create a chart similar to the example below and have the students fill in the information.

3. After completing the chart, discuss how the order of the various scenes directed the story.

4. Brainstorm additional locations the baby and family could visit. How could the story be extended? How would new locations affect the order of the story?

5. Have students keep a log of where they go during the course of the day for several days. Does their routine vary? How are their weekend routines different? How would variance in their weekend routines affect a story about their routines in general?

Scene Location	Characters in Scene	Event
1. Bedroom	Baby, parents, grandmother	Baby is sleeping.
2. Bedroom	Baby, parents, grandmother	Baby is crying. Adults running to the baby.

From: Bridges to Reading, Grades K–3: Teaching Reading Skills with Children's Literature. © 1999 Suzanne I. Barchers. Teacher Ideas Press (800) 237-6124.

Related books

Curtis, Jamie Lee. *Tell Me Again About the Night I Was Born.* Illustrated by Laura Cornell. New York: HarperCollins, 1996.

Voake, Charlotte. *Mr. Davies and the Baby.* Cambridge, Mass.: Candlewick Press, 1996.

Waddell, Martin. *Once There Were Giants.* Illustrated by Penny Dale. Cambridge, Mass.: Candlewick Press, 1995.

From: Bridges to Reading, Grades K-3: Teaching Reading Skills with Children's Literature. © 1999 Suzanne I. Barchers. Teacher Ideas Press (800) 237-6124.

Lansky, Bruce. *The New Adventures of Mother Goose: Gentle Rhymes for Happy Times.* Illustrated by Stephen Carpenter. Deephaven, Minn.: Meadowbrook Press, 1993.

Grade levels: 2–3.

When Little Miss Muffet eats an ice cream cone and tells the spider to go get his own, you know you are reading an unusual nursery rhyme. Lansky creates new rhymes that invite participation through the lively pictures and predictable verse. Children of all ages will enjoy these amusing rhymes.

Activities

1. Read a variety of rhymes aloud but save some of the rhymes for activity 3 below. Pause during the reading of the last line and let the students fill in how they think the rhyme will end. Encourage them to read the pictures to help them predict the rhymes.

2. After reading a variety of the rhymes, ask the students to recite some traditional nursery rhymes that they know. Write those versions and Lansky's on the board or on chart paper and compare them. Explain that Lansky's rhyme can be called a parody, an amusing new version of the traditional poem.

3. Using one of the resources listed below or any collection of traditional nursery rhymes, choose several that Lansky has revised and read the traditional versions aloud. Create parodies as a class or in small groups. Encourage the students to be creative in their parodies. Then read aloud Lansky's version. Did their new rhymes turn out as good as or better than Lansky's?

4. List a variety of nursery rhyme characters on the board. What would happen if they interacted? For example, Peter Pumpkin Eater could meet up with Mary Quite Contrary and try to steal a pumpkin from her garden. Create new rhymes that involve several characters. Put them together into a new book, making a second copy for the library's use.

Related books

Mother Goose or the Old Nursery Rhymes. Illustrated by Kate Greenaway. New York: Merrimack, n. d.

The Real Mother Goose. Illustrated by Blanche Fisher Wright. Chicago: Rand McNally, 1944.

Wyndham, Robert, editor. *Chinese Mother Goose Rhymes.* Illustrated by Ed Young. New York: Philomel, 1968.

From: Bridges to Reading, Grades K-3: Teaching Reading Skills with Children's Literature. © 1999 Suzanne I. Barchers. Teacher Ideas Press (800) 237-6124.

Literary Elements and Features: Personification

Kirk, David. *Miss Spider's Tea Party.* New York: Scholastic, 1994.

Grade levels: K–1.

Miss Spider sips her tea and longs to have friends. She asks a variety of guests to join her: two beetles, three fireflies, four bumblebees, five rubber bugs, six ants, seven butterflies, and nine moths. But they all decline. After she helps a wet moth dry out, the moth tells the others that she is harmless, and they all join her for tea.

Activities

1. Although the word *personification* may be difficult for children in grades kindergarten and 1 to understand, they can begin to appreciate the difference between a book in which animals talk and act like humans and one in which they exhibit their true behaviors. Read *Miss Spider's Tea Party* aloud. Then make up a chart that chronicles the events in the story. Have the students decide if the events could really happen or if they are things only humans do and thereby examples of personification. Consider the example below as a starting place for your discussion.

2. Compare this story with other stories students know about spiders. Do these stories contain examples of personification, too? What other books use personification?

Event in Story	Realistic or Personification
Spider sipping tea	Personification
Insects flying by	Realistic
Spider talking	Personification
Spider serving tea	Personification

Related books

Carle, Eric. *The Very Busy Spider.* New York: Philomel, 1985.

Kirk, David. *Miss Spider's Wedding.* New York: Scholastic, 1995.

From: Bridges to Reading, Grades K–3: Teaching Reading Skills with Children's Literature. © 1999 Suzanne I. Barchers. Teacher Ideas Press (800) 237-6124.

Van Allsburg, Chris. *The Z Was Zapped.* Boston: Houghton Mifflin, 1987.

Grade levels: 2–3.

This "Play in Twenty-Six Acts" features all 26 letters of the alphabet. On each right-hand page, something is happening to the letter on the stage. The readers can guess at what is happening, predicting the line that follows when the page is turned. For example, rocks are falling on the letter *A,* predicting an avalanche.

Activities

1. Share the book, allowing the students to predict what is happening to each letter. After finishing the book, discuss the tone of the book, asking the students how they feel about the portrayal of the letters.

2. Discuss how the letters have been personified in the book: cut to ribbons, nearly drowned, evaporating. Make a list of the letters and identify the features, when obvious, that illustrate personification.

3. Compare this book with other alphabet books. Do other books also use personification or do they use objects in a more typical fashion?

4. Have students work in small groups to create their own alphabet book, using Van Allsburg's book as a model. Give each group a few letters to develop, incorporating human emotions or features. For example, the book could start with the letter *A* being addled or appalled. Encourage the students who enjoy illustrating to draw the letters with features that show the personification. Collect the examples into a book, setting it up in the same fashion with opportunities for prediction. Share the book with another class. How well do they predict the events?

Related books

Isadora, Rachel. *City Seen from A to Z.* New York: Trumpet, 1983.

Kitamura, Satoshi. *From Acorn to Zoo and Everything in Between in Alphabetical Order.* New York: Trumpet, 1992.

Pallotta, Jerry. *The Dinosaur Alphabet Book.* Illustrated by Ralph Masiello. New York: Trumpet, 1991.

———. *The Yucky Reptile Alphabet Book.* Illustrated by Ralph Masiello. New York: Trumpet, 1989.

From: Bridges to Reading, Grades K–3: Teaching Reading Skills with Children's Literature. © 1999 Suzanne I. Barchers. Teacher Ideas Press (800) 237-6124.

From: Bridges to Reading, Grades K–3: Teaching Reading Skills with Children's Literature. © 1999 Suzanne I. Barchers. Teacher Ideas Press (800) 237-6124.

Blumenthal, Deborah. *The Chocolate-Covered-Cookie Tantrum.* Illustrated by Harvey Stevenson. New York: Clarion, 1996.

Grade levels: K–1.

Sophie and her mother are on their way home from the park when Sophie sees a girl eating a chocolate-covered cookie. It looks so delicious that Sophie insists she should have one—immediately. Her mother tells her that she doesn't have one and that it is almost time for supper, but Sophie persists until she has a full-blown tantrum. After a nap and supper, Sophie finally enjoys a chocolate-covered cookie.

Activities

1. Before reading the story, ask the students if they have ever wanted a treat just before supper. Did an adult tell them they had to wait until after their meal to have the treat? Did they get angry when they couldn't have it? Discuss how they felt when they disagreed with the adult. Explain that this type of disagreement is called a conflict and that it occurs in the book you are going to read.

2. Read aloud the book, taking time to discuss the way the pictures show the increasing frustration when Sophie can't have a chocolate-covered cookie.

3. Ask the students how Sophie's mother tried to resolve the conflict. Could they think of other ways to resolve the conflict? Why do they think Sophie got so out of control? Should Sophie's mother have found a cookie for Sophie or made her wait until after dinner? Have the students ever been so tired that they acted up more than usual?

4. Ask the students if they think Sophie should have gotten a cookie after supper. Discuss how the conflict between Sophie and her mother developed and how we often face conflicts when our wants don't agree with those of our parents.

Related books

Bush, Timothy. *James in the House of Aunt Prudence.* New York: Crown, 1993.

Kamish, Daniel, and David Kamish. *The Night the Scary Beasties Popped Out of My Head.* New York: Random House, 1998.

Moss, Miriam. *The Snoops.* Illustrated by Delphine Durand. New York: Dutton, 1997.

Laden, Nina. *Private I. Guana: The Case of the Missing Chameleon.* San Francisco: Chronicle, 1995.

Grade levels: 2–3.

Private I. Guana sets out to find a missing chameleon. Liz fears that her husband, Leon, is in trouble. At first Private I. Guana is unsuccessful in his search for Leon, but then he wanders into the Lizard Lounge in search of fried grasshoppers and becomes entranced with a singer. Happily, he discovers the entertainer is Leon, singing in disguise.

Activities

1. Ask the students if they have ever read a mystery. Do they know what a private investigator does? Discuss the job of a private investigator or detective.

2. Begin reading the story aloud to the students, stopping after reading the page about I. Guana getting tired and having no clues. Ask the students what the conflict is so far in the story. Draw out the fact that there is a missing chameleon and that the private investigator has no clues or leads as to his whereabouts.

3. After reading the next page, when Private I. Guana spots the Lizard Lounge, discuss the conflict he experiences: His head tells him not to go there, but his stomach wants some fried grasshoppers. Ask the students how they think he will resolve this conflict.

4. Continue reading the book. After finishing it, discuss the conflict that Leon had. Could Leon have thought of other ways to resolve his desire to perform with being married and suspecting that Liz thought he was boring. How did Leon eventually resolve his conflict?

5. Discuss how the style of this book is a takeoff on the private detective radio shows of the past. If possible, share a recording of "The Shadow" or another old-time radio show and compare it with the book.

Related books

Conford, Ellen. *A Case for Jenny Archer.* Illustrated by Diane Palmisciano. Boston: Little, Brown, 1988.

Cushman, Doug. *The Mystery of King Karfu.* New York: HarperCollins, 1996.

———. *The Mystery of the Monkey's Maze.* New York: HarperCollins, 1999.

From: Bridges to Reading, Grades K–3: Teaching Reading Skills with Children's Literature. © 1999 Suzanne I. Barchers. Teacher Ideas Press (800) 237-6124.

From: Bridges to Reading, Grades K–3: Teaching Reading Skills with Children's Literature. © 1999 Suzanne I. Barchers. Teacher Ideas Press (800) 237-6124.

 Scieszka, Jon. *The True Story of the 3 Little Pigs.* Illustrated by Lane Smith. New York: Viking Penguin, 1989.

Grade levels: K–1.

In this story told by A. Wolf, the reader learns that the wolf was making a birthday cake for his granny when he ran out of sugar. He went down the street to a neighbor's, only to sneeze so much with his cold that the pig's house blew down. Because the pig was dead, he claims, he couldn't help but eat him. Finally, A. Wolf is captured at the third pig's house. The real story, Wolf maintains, is that he was framed.

Activities

1. Ask the students to tell the story of the three little pigs as they have heard it. If they have trouble recalling it, briefly retell the traditional story.

2. Read the book aloud, allowing the students to enjoy the humorous pictures. Note the details, such as the picture of granny, who looks suspiciously like the wolf from *Little Red Riding Hood.*

3. Make a list of key points in the plot of this book and another list of those in the traditional story. Compare the lists. Which details are the same and which are different?

4. Explain the term *point of view* and discuss how the wolf's story is very different from that of the pigs'. Ask the students if they recall times when their point of view was different from someone else's (e.g., wanting to stay up late when their parents wanted them to go to bed; wanting to have another cookie; having a different opinion from a sibling regarding the reasons for a fight).

5. Write a newspaper report based on the wolf's capture from the pigs' point of view. Create a rebuttal letter written by the wolf.

Related books

Dahl, Roald. *Roald Dahl's Revolting Rhymes.* Illustrated by Quentin Blake. New York: Bantam Books, 1986.

Kellogg, Steven. *The Three Little Pigs.* New York: Morrow, 1997.

Trivizas, Eugene. *The Three Little Wolves and the Big Bad Pig.* Illustrated by Helen Oxenbury. New York: Macmillan, 1993.

Blume, Judy. *The Pain and the Great One.* Illustrated by Irene Trivas. Scarsdale, N.Y.: Bradbury Press, 1974, 1984.

Grade levels: 2–3.

An older sister describes what a pain her brother is. Her mother has to carry him into the kitchen for breakfast; he gets to be first at everything; he picks at his food and still gets dessert; and it's clear her parents love him best. In the second half of the book, the younger brother describes how his older sister thinks she's so great. She's older; she can play real songs on the piano; she can baby-sit; and it's clear her parents love her best.

Activities

1. Ask the students how many brothers and sisters they have. Do they ever feel like their parents love the sibling best? Read the sister's portion of the book aloud. Stop the reading and ask the students if they have ever had similar feelings toward a younger sibling. Then read the rest of the book. Have they had those feelings about an older sibling?

2. Discuss how the author explored each of the children's feelings by writing from each one's point of view. Make a list of the characteristics of each sibling that proved annoying to the other one. Then ask students to think of characteristics that annoy them about their siblings. If they don't have a sibling, have them think about another family member. List their responses on the board.

3. Have the students write a personal list of characteristics about themselves that might annoy someone else. Encourage the students to be honest, emphasizing that their lists will not be shared publicly. When the students have made their lists, allow them to tear them up and throw them away, symbolizing the shedding of annoying habits. Encourage them to think about how another person's point of view may be different from their own.

Related books

Krause, Robert. *Little Louie the Baby Bloomer.* Illustrated by Jose Aruego and Ariane Dewey. New York: HarperCollins, 1998.

Lerner, Harriet, and Susan Goldhor. *What's So Terrible About Swallowing an Apple Seed?* Illustrated by Catharine O'Neill. New York: HarperCollins, 1996.

Schwartz, Amy. *A Teeny Tiny Baby.* New York: Orchard, 1994.

From: Bridges to Reading, Grades K–3: Teaching Reading Skills with Children's Literature. © 1999 Suzanne I. Barchers. Teacher Ideas Press (800) 237-6124.

From: Bridges to Reading, Grades K–3: Teaching Reading Skills with Children's Literature. © 1999 Suzanne I. Barchers. Teacher Ideas Press (800) 237-6124.

Literary Elements and Features: Realism Versus Fantasy

Greenstein, Elaine. *Mattie's Hats Won't Wear That!* New York: Alfred A. Knopf, 1997.

Grade levels: K–1.

Mattie loves making whimsical creations in her hat shop. Although people enjoy looking at her hats, they rarely buy them. The night after the mail carrier delivers an odd assortment of hat adornments, the hats rebel, taking off their ornaments. But the hats find that people miss the decorated hats. Mattie leaves the ornaments out one night, and the hats decorate themselves. The hats soon are sold to happy customers, leading Mattie to let the hats choose their own adornments.

Activities

1. Read the book aloud. Ask the students to identify what is real and what is pretend or fantasy in the story.

2. Make a chart such as the one below. As you reread the story, list the events in the appropriate category.

3. Have the students bring in old hats and a variety of unusual adornments. Have them make new, unusual hats. Encourage them to wear the hats during creative play.

Real	Fantasy
Mattie makes unusual hats.	
People look at the hats but don't buy them.	
The mail carrier brings new ornaments.	
	The beret peeks inside the box and tears off the planet Saturn from his stem.
	The hats take off all their ornaments.

67

Literary Elements and Features: Realism Versus Fantasy

Related books

Fleming, Candace. *The Hatmaker's Sign.* Illustrated by Robert Andrew Parker. New York: Orchard, 1998.

Ketteman, Helen. *Aunt Hilarity's Bustle.* Illustrated by James Warhola. New York: Simon & Schuster, 1992.

Sharples, Joseph. *The Flyaway Pantaloons.* Illustrated by Sue Scullard. Minneapolis, Minn.: Carolrhoda Books, 1990.

From: Bridges to Reading, Grades K-3: Teaching Reading Skills with Children's Literature. © 1999 Suzanne I. Barchers. Teacher Ideas Press (800) 237-6124.

Thompson, Colin. *How to Live Forever.* New York: Alfred A. Knopf, 1995.

Grade levels: 2–3.

In this story, the shelves in the library come to life at night. A young boy who lives in a cookbook sets out in search of a book entitled *How to Live Forever.* When he finally discovers the truth, he learns that living forever brings an unexpected set of problems. He then faces a dilemma: Does he want to live forever?

Activities

1. Read the story aloud, allowing time for the students to savor the pictures. Pause at the point where Peter stops to watch the goldfish, near the end of the story. Ask the students what they think Peter will do. Make two columns on the board as illustrated below. Discuss the students' ideas and then finish the book. Some reasons could logically appear in both categories.

2. Read the book again. Discuss the story's realistic aspects, such as its setting in a library. Then discuss the fantasy of the library coming to life and living forever. Discuss other settings where this story could have taken place (e.g., a museum, a closet, a playroom). Ask the students why they think the author chose to set the story in a library.

3. Collect other books that combine fantasy and realism from the "Related books" list below. (Older students will appreciate Natalie Babbitt's *Tuck Everlasting,* a chapter book that addresses the dilemma of living forever.) Read the books aloud. How are they alike, and how are they different from this book?

Reasons to Live Forever	Reasons Not to Live Forever
You would always be young.	Your friends would grow up and go away.
You would never die.	You would be "frozen in time."

From: Bridges to Reading, Grades K–3: Teaching Reading Skills with Children's Literature. © 1999 Suzanne I. Barchers. Teacher Ideas Press (800) 237-6124.

Literary Elements and Features: Realism Versus Fantasy

Related books

Babbitt, Natalie. *Tuck Everlasting.* New York: Farrar, Straus & Giroux, 1975.

Clement, Rod. *Just Another Ordinary Day.* New York: HarperCollins, 1995.

Paz, Octavio. *My Life with the Wave.* Translated by Catherine Cowan. Illustrated by Mark Buehner. New York: Lothrop, Lee and Shepard, 1997.

Sendak, Maurice. *Outside Over There.* New York: Harper & Row, 1981.

————. *Where the Wild Things Are.* New York: Harper & Row, 1963.

From: Bridges to Reading, Grades K-3: Teaching Reading Skills with Children's Literature. © 1999 Suzanne I. Barchers. Teacher Ideas Press (800) 237-6124.

Crebbin, June. *Into the Castle.* Illustrated by John Bendall-Brunello. Cambridge, Mass.: Candlewick Press, 1996.

Grade levels: K–1.

Three children, a dog, and a horse set off on a journey to a castle. Each double-page spread shows a new setting: on the hill, at the moat, on the drawbridge, in the yard, in a passage. The story reverses as they flee the castle and the monster whom they have inadvertently freed. At the end, the monster thanks them for letting him out.

Activities

1. Read the book aloud. If the class has discussed prepositions, reinforce the use of prepositions throughout the story.

2. Make a list of all the places the characters are shown in, starting with the hillside.

3. Explain to the students that they are going to draw a story circle that shows the settings of the story. Give the students a large piece of paper. Give them a pattern so that they can draw a large circle on the paper. Outside the circle and at the top, begin by writing the first setting: *on the hillside.* Then ask the students to think ahead to the middle of the story when they free the monster. Where is that setting? Have them write *in the dungeon* at the outside bottom of the circle.

4. Reread the first part of the book and decide how to divide the circle to write each of the settings the characters experience after the hillside on the right side of the circle between the top and the bottom. Then continue around the circle, writing the settings they experience as they leave the castle until they have completed the circle and are on the hillside again at the top of the circle. The students could then draw a picture of the monster inside the circle.

Related books

Dematons, Charlotte. *Looking for Cinderella.* Arden, N.C.: Front Street, 1996.

Galdone, Paul. *Jack and the Beanstalk.* New York: Clarion, 1974.

Kimmel, Eric A. *The Gingerbread Man.* Illustrated by Megan Lloyd. New York: Holiday House, 1993.

From: Bridges to Reading, Grades K–3: Teaching Reading Skills with Children's Literature. © 1999 Suzanne I. Barchers. Teacher Ideas Press (800) 237-6124.

Literary Elements and Features: Setting

French, Vivian. *Lazy Jack.* Illustrated by Russell Ayto. Cambridge, Mass.: Candlewick Press, 1995.

Grade levels: 2–3.

Lazy Jack's mother decides Jack must go to work. He works for a builder but loses the coin he is paid. His mother tells him he should have put it in his pocket. The next day he works for a farmer, and when he is paid a jug of milk, he pours it in his pocket. His mother tells him he should have carried it on his head. His misadventures continue until his antics amuse everyone so much that he is given all that the pair need.

Activities

1. Read the story aloud, encouraging the students to predict what Jack will do with his pay each time.

2. Read the story again. This time ask the students to note all the different places Jack goes to, such as the builder's site, the farm, and the dairy. List the settings on the board.

3. Tell the students that they are going to create a story stair that shows the settings. To begin, draw a simple profile of a staircase on the board. At the first step, write *Jack's home.* Then ask the students what should go on the second step: *the builder's site.* Keep adding the settings until they have reconstructed the story.

4. Some of the students may have heard other versions of this folk tale. Allow them to share any variants they know, creating another story stair if possible.

5. Brainstorm new places Jack might work and how he might get paid, creating a variant called *Lazy Jack, Continued.*

Related books

Sierra, Judy, and Robert Kaminski. "Lazy Jack." In *MultiCultural Folktales: Stories to Tell Young Children,* p. 109. Phoenix, Ariz.: Oryx Press, 1991.

Yolen, Jane, ed. "Lazy Jack." In *Favorite Folktales from Around the World,* p. 176. New York: Pantheon, 1986.

From: Bridges to Reading, Grades K–3: Teaching Reading Skills with Children's Literature. © 1999 Suzanne I. Barchers. Teacher Ideas Press (800) 237-6124.

French, Vivian. *Aesop's Funky Fables.* Illustrated by Korky Paul. New York: Viking, 1997.

Grade levels: 2–3.

Although the main element of each of the 10 fables remains the same, each has been told with a fresh spin. For example, "The Dog and the Bone" is told in a lean verse form. "The Hare and the Tortoise" features repetitive verses, along with many examples of onomatopoeia. The fanciful illustrations enliven the innovative retellings.

Activities

1. Begin by reading two or three traditional versions of a familiar fable, such as "The Hare and the Tortoise." Then read French's version, sharing the illustrations. Discuss how the treatments differ. Which do the students prefer?

2. Repeat this process with another familiar fable. Discuss the message of the fable. Did the new treatment change the message, or is the moral still clear? Share other fables and discuss French's treatments.

3. Read a variety of Arnold Lobel's fables (see entry in the "Related books" section below). Compare the versions he writes. How do they compare with the traditional stories?

4. Read traditional versions of "The Fox and the Crow." Next read French's version. Then use the readers theatre script on page 74. How does this script compare with the other versions?

5. Choose other fables and have groups of students transform them into readers theatre scripts. Designate a day to share the scripts among the students.

Related books

Calmenson, Stephanie. *The Children's Aesop.* Illustrated by Robert Byrd. Honesdale, Penn.: Boyds Mills Press, 1992.

Carle, Eric. *Twelve Tales From Aesop.* New York: Philomel, 1980.

Galdone, Paul. *Three Aesop Fox Fables.* New York: Clarion, 1971.

Heins, Ethel. *The Cat and the Cook and Other Fables of Krylov.* Illustrated by Anita Lobel. New York: Greenwillow, 1995.

Lobel, Arnold. *Fables.* New York: Harper & Row, 1980.

From: Bridges to Reading, Grades K–3: Teaching Reading Skills with Children's Literature. © 1999 Suzanne I. Barchers. Teacher Ideas Press (800) 237-6124.

THE FOX AND THE CROW

Narrator: One day a fox saw a crow fly by. The crow had a piece of cheese in its beak. Seeing the cheese made the fox very hungry. The crow came to rest on the branch of a tree.

Fox: Good morning, crow. Will you share your cheese with me?

Narrator: The crow looked at the fox. It slowly shook its head.

Fox: You look so kind. I am so hungry. Please share with me.

Narrator: The crow looked at the fox. Again it slowly shook its head.

Fox: You are the finest crow I have ever seen. Your feathers are so black and glossy. You also have good luck by getting that cheese. Won't you share your good fortune with me?

Narrator: The crow looked at the fox. Again it slowly shook its head.

Fox: Your eyes are so bright. I am sure your voice must be every bit as beautiful. Won't you sing for me? Then I will greet you as the Ruler of Birds.

Narrator: The crow could not resist such flattery.

Crow: Caw, caw, caw.

Narrator: As the crow sang, the cheese dropped to the ground. The fox gobbled it up.

Crow: You are a sneaky beast. One day your tricks will get you into trouble. You should be taught a lesson.

Fox: That may be true. But you have learned a valuable lesson, crow. *Do not trust a fox that flatters!*

From *Fifty Fabulous Fables.* © 1997 Suzanne I. Barchers. Teacher Ideas Press. (800) 237-6124.

From: Bridges to Reading, Grades K-3: Teaching Reading Skills with Children's Literature. © 1999 Suzanne I. Barchers. Teacher Ideas Press (800) 237-6124.

From: Bridges to Reading, Grades K–3: Teaching Reading Skills with Children's Literature. © 1999 Suzanne I. Barchers. Teacher Ideas Press (800) 237-6124.

Dematons, Charlotte. *Looking for Cinderella.* Arden, N.C.: Front Street, 1996.

Grade levels: 2–3.

One day, after noticing something different about the nearby windmill, Hilda goes for a walk. She finds herself a victim of mistaken identity as she is drawn into a land of stories. No one wants to believe that she is not Cinderella, so she decides she will have to find her. Hilda finally discovers Cinderella, ensuring that the story will continue as it should.

Activities

1. Just as characters in most fairy tales, Hilda faced a variety of obstacles. List the obstacles on the board. Compare these with those in the traditional story of Cinderella, perhaps constructing a chart similar to the following:

Cinderella's Obstacles	Hilda's Obstacles
Stepsisters	Characters identifying her as Cinderella
Not having a dress for the ball	Meeting a witch

2. Repeat the process with other characters, identifying how each character overcame the obstacles. Which character showed more initiative?

3. Create additional obstacles that could be used to develop another spin-off. For example, create a version that develops the prince's efforts to find Cinderella. He might face a dragon or a wizard, among others. Write the stories in small groups and complete them with illustrations. Create a section in the class library dedicated to spin-offs.

Literary Elements and Features: Spin-Offs

Related books

Climo, Shirley. *The Egyptian Cinderella.* Illustrated by Ruth Heller. New York: Harper-Collins, 1989.

———. *The Irish Cinderlad.* Illustrated by Loretta Krupinski. New York: HarperCollins, 1996.

———. *The Korean Cinderella.* Illustrated by Ruth Heller. New York: HarperCollins, 1993.

Martin, Rafe. *The Rough-Face Girl.* Illustrated by David Shannon. New York: G. P. Putnam's Sons, 1992.

Minters, Frances. *Cinder-Elly.* Illustrated by G. Brian Karas. New York: Viking, 1994.

Sierra, Judy. *Cinderella.* Phoenix, Ariz.: Oryx Press, 1992.

From: Bridges to Reading, Grades K–3: Teaching Reading Skills with Children's Literature. © 1999 Suzanne I. Barchers. Teacher Ideas Press (800) 237-6124.

From: Bridges to Reading, Grades K–3: Teaching Reading Skills with Children's Literature. © 1999 Suzanne I. Barchers. Teacher Ideas Press (800) 237-6124.

Bush, Timothy. *James in the House of Aunt Prudence.* New York: Crown, 1993.

Grade levels: K–1.

When James goes to visit his great-aunt Prudence, he yearns for a tour of the house. While she is busy writing a letter, James sets out on an adventure. A bear arrives, and they end up fighting with the Mouse King. Soon the entire house joins the fight, creating chaos. When Great-Aunt Prudence finishes her letter, she fixes up the bear and they continue the fun.

Activities

1. Read the story aloud to the students without showing them the pictures. When finished, ask the students what they liked about the story. How did it make them feel? Excited? Anxious? Wishing that they could have such an adventure?

2. Reread the story, this time showing the illustrations. What are the students' reactions to the story now? Did they find it more exciting with the illustrations?

3. Explain to the students that this author also created the illustrations for the book. How do the illustrations contribute to the story?

4. Discuss how the author wrote the story in a simple style, choosing his words very carefully. For example, what did the students think of when they heard the phrases *fought valiantly* or *in hot pursuit?* If the author hadn't created such rich illustrations, would he have had to create a more complicated story to explain what was happening?

5. Discuss other books that have distinctive styles, such as those found in the "Related books" section below. Compare the use of words with the illustrations.

Related books

Blumenthal, Deborah. *The Chocolate-Covered-Cookie Tantrum.* Illustrated by Harvey Stevenson. New York: Clarion, 1996.

Kamish, Daniel, and David Kamish. *The Night the Scary Beasties Popped out of My Head.* New York: Random House, 1998.

Martin, Linda. *When Dinosaurs Go Visiting.* San Francisco: Chronicle, 1993.

Moss, Miriam. *The Snoops.* Illustrated by Delphine Durand. New York: Dutton, 1997.

Moss, Miriam. *The Snoops.* Illustrated by Delphine Durand. New York: Dutton, 1997.

Grade levels: 2–3.

The Snoops, who live at number nine Keyhole Place, love to mind everyone's business. They pry into other people's lives, taking note of everything they do and say. At the same time, they fear that someone else will snoop on them. Of course, the entire neighborhood plots to do exactly that, providing readers with an outrageous ending and an opportunity to do their own snooping.

Activities

1. Ask the students if they ever play detective, snoop into a sibling's room or drawers, or pry into someone else's business. Discuss how snooping can sometimes be harmless and sometimes be an intrusion into someone's privacy. Tell the students that this book is about some outrageous snoops who love to mind everyone else's business.

2. Read the book aloud. Pass the book around at the end of the story, giving everyone time to look through the keyhole on the last page.

3. Return to the beginning of the book. Reread the first page. Discuss the phrases the author uses to describe the Snoops' behaviors. Discuss how her careful selection of phrases shows her style.

4. On the next page, point out the words that are larger. What impact do these words have on the style of the author's writing?

5. As you continue with the second reading, note the use of alliteration. Discuss how using alliteration makes the style fun to read and listen to. (Other devices the author uses includes rhyme and onomatopoeia.)

6. Finally, discuss how the illustrations support the zany style of the story.

Related books

Conford, Ellen. *A Case for Jenny Archer.* Illustrated by Diane Palmisciano. Boston: Little, Brown, 1988.

Cushman, Doug. *The Mystery of King Karfu.* New York: HarperCollins, 1996.

Laden, Nina. *Private I. Guana: The Case of the Missing Chameleon.* San Francisco: Chronicle, 1995.

From: Bridges to Reading, Grades K–3: Teaching Reading Skills with Children's Literature. © 1999 Suzanne I. Barchers. Teacher Ideas Press (800) 237-6124.

From: *Bridges to Reading, Grades K–3: Teaching Reading Skills with Children's Literature.* © 1999 Suzanne I. Barchers. Teacher Ideas Press (800) 237-6124.

McCully, Emily Arnold. *Mirette on the High Wire.* New York: Putnam, 1992, 1997.

Grade levels: 2–3.

Mirette lives with her widowed mother in Paris in the late 1800s. Famous people come to stay in their boardinghouse, including Bellini, a retired high-wire walker. Mirette begins practicing on the wire, and Bellini begins to teach her. When he confesses that he has become afraid of the high wire, Mirette inspires him to overcome his fear.

Activities

1. Read the book aloud to the students. Find Paris on a map or globe and discuss the culture that fostered many artists, musicians, and performers near the turn of the century. Note the style of the illustrations throughout this award-winning book.

2. Tell the students that there are actually two stories in the book and that you are going to read the book again so that they can identify both stories. Reread the book.

3. Ask the students who the two main characters are (Bellini and Mirette). Then ask them to summarize each of their stories. Then draw parallels between the stories, such as in the example below.

4. Discuss the fact that many stories have subplots. Do the students agree that Mirette's story is the main one and that Bellini's overcoming of his fear is the subplot? The class may decide that both characters' stories are equally important to the whole story. Compare this book with others that have subplots.

Mirette's Story	Bellini's Story
Mirette sees Bellini on the high wire.	Bellini was a famous high-wire walker.
Mirette wants to learn the high wire.	Bellini practices on the high wire.
Mirette practices on her own.	Bellini decides to teach her.
Mirette learns of Bellini's fame.	Bellini confesses his fear.

Literary Elements and Features: Subplots

Related books

Ehrlich, Amy. *Lucy's Winter Tale.* Illustrated by Troy Howell. New York: Dial, 1992.

Fleming, Candace. *The Hatmaker's Sign: A Story by Benjamin Franklin.* Illustrated by Robert Andrew Parker. New York: Orchard, 1998.

Williams, Karen Lynn. *Painted Dreams.* Illustrated by Catherine Stock. New York: Lothrop, Lee and Shepard, 1998.

From: Bridges to Reading, Grades K-3: Teaching Reading Skills with Children's Literature. © 1999 Suzanne I. Barchers: Teacher Ideas Press (800) 237-6124.

From: Bridges to Reading, Grades K–3: Teaching Reading Skills with Children's Literature. © 1999 Suzanne I. Barchers. Teacher Ideas Press (800) 237-6124.

 Gershator, Phillis. *Sweet, Sweet Fig Banana.* Illustrated by Fritz Millevoix. Morton Grove, Ill.: Whitman, 1996.

Grade levels: K–1.

Soto has planted fig bananas in his yard in the Virgin Islands. One day he and his mother go to the market, where he is given a hat and a fraico (flavored ice shavings). He is also helped by the librarian. When his bananas have ripened, he and his mother sell all but three hands of bananas, which he gives to his benefactors.

Activities

1. Begin reading the book aloud, allowing time to appreciate the illustrations of the colorful island. Stop reading at the page where Soto's mother gives him the bananas. Ask the students what they think Soto is going to do with them. Accept all reasonable answers as possibilities.

2. After reading the remainder of the story, discuss why Soto wanted to give away the bananas when he could have sold them for money. Discuss how the theme of the story was the kindnesses done to Soto and how he was able to return a favor to his friends.

3. Ask the students if they have ever been surprised when someone did something especially nice for them. Think of times when people, such as the school secretary, principal, janitor, or another teacher, have been helpful to the class. Plan something to show a kindness in return, such as making a treat or a card.

4. On May Day, people used to anonymously leave baskets of flowers on neighbors' porches. Plan a day when the students can anonymously surprise selected friends or school personnel. Plan on keeping the event secret.

Related books

Lies, Brian. *Hamlet and the Enormous Chinese Dragon Kite.* Boston: Houghton Mifflin, 1994.

Paraskevas, Betty, and Michael Paraskevas. *The Tangerine Bear.* New York: HarperCollins, 1997.

Reiser, Lynn. *Cherry Pies and Lullabies.* New York: Greenwillow, 1998.

Shannon, George. *Heart to Heart.* Illustrated by Steve Björkman. Boston: Houghton Mifflin, 1995.

Stevens, Jan Romero. *Carlos and the Squash Plant.* Illustrated by Jeanne Arnold. Flagstaff, Ariz.: Northland, 1993. (In both English and Spanish.)

Grade levels: 2–3.

Carlos refuses to wash his ears, despite his mother's warning that if he doesn't wash, a squash plant will grow in them. Soon a squash plant *does* grow in his ears. Carlos has to go to great lengths to hide the plant, including wearing a huge hat. Finally, he decides to wash his ears during his bath, and the plant disappears.

Activities

1. Ask the students if they have ever been told that if they swallow an apple seed a tree will grow in their stomachs, or if they swallow a watermelon seed a watermelon will grow. Explain that you are going to read a book about a little boy who disobeys his mother, refusing to wash his ears. Ask if they can predict what might happen.

2. After reading the book aloud, discuss how the author used a boy's disobedience to develop her story. Can the students think of other warnings that, when ignored, could become the basis for an amusing story? ("If you frown like that, your face will freeze." "Eat your carrots. They'll improve your eyesight.") Work together as a class to create a group story or have small groups write a story in which a youngster is disobedient.

3. Discuss how folk tales, such as *Little Red Riding Hood,* use such themes as warnings. They are called "cautionary tales," warning children not to speak to strangers or stray off the path. Investigate other folk tales that encourage appropriate behavior, for example, *Hansel and Gretel, The Little Red Hen,* and *Goldilocks and the Three Bears.*

Related books

Bluementhal, Deborah. *The Chocolate-Covered-Cookie Tantrum.* Illustrated by Harvey Stevenson. New York: Clarion, 1996.

Heo, Yumi. *The Green Frogs.* Boston: Houghton Mifflin, 1996.

Jeram, Anita. *Contrary Mary.* Cambridge, Mass.: Candlewick Press, 1995.

Lerner, Harriet, and Susan Goldhor. *What's So Terrible About Swallowing an Apple Seed?* Illustrated by Catharine O'Neill. New York: HarperCollins, 1996.

From: Bridges to Reading, Grades K–3: Teaching Reading Skills with Children's Literature. © 1999 Suzanne I. Barchers. Teacher Ideas Press (800) 237-6124.

Isadora, Rachel. *A South African Night.* New York: Greenwillow, 1998.

Grade levels: K–1.

When night comes to Johannesburg, South Africa, the people go to sleep. But the animals stir, hunting for food, grazing in the fields, and drinking at the water hole. When the sun comes up, the animals prepare to sleep while the people prepare for a new day. Colorful illustrations set the tone for this simple, beautiful book.

Activities

1. Find Johannesburg on a map. Ask the students what they know about South Africa. Discuss where it is in relation to your community.

2. Read the book aloud. Then read the book again, stopping at every page or two. Ask the students how the text and illustrations make them feel. Does the city look busy and exciting? Does the little girl in bed make them feel peaceful? Is the black mamba snake scary?

3. Discuss how the feeling or tone of the book changes, depending on the illustrations and the topic. Because this may be one of their first experiences with discussing the tone of a book, do not go into great detail. Just discuss what the students think about when they see and hear the story.

4. Compare the book with other books found in the "Related books" section below. Do others have a similar tone? Can the students think of books that are especially different from this one? How does the tone of these books differ?

Related books

Brown, Margaret Wise. *Little Donkey Close Your Eyes.* Illustrated by Ashley Wolff. New York: HarperCollins, 1959, 1987, 1995.

Cowcher, Helen. *Tigress.* New York: Farrar, Straus & Giroux, 1991.

Fox, Mem. *Time for Bed.* Illustrated by Jane Dyer. New York: Trumpet, 1993.

Lewison, Wendy Cheyette. *Going to Sleep on the Farm.* Illustrated by Juan Wijngaard. New York: Trumpet, 1994.

From: Bridges to Reading, Grades K–3: Teaching Reading Skills with Children's Literature. © 1999 Suzanne I. Barchers. Teacher Ideas Press (800) 237-6124.

Literary Elements and Features: Tone

 Deedy, Carmen Agra. *The Library Dragon.* Illustrated by Michael P. White. Atlanta, Ga.: Peachtree, 1994.

Grade levels: 2–3.

Miss Lotta Scales, a well-intentioned dragon, knew she was ideal for the job of librarian at Sunrise Elementary School. However, her enthusiasm for protecting the books meant that the children didn't get to use them. It takes the courage of one youngster to break the spell and turn the dragon into a children- and book-loving librarian.

Activities

1. Read the story aloud. Discuss the fanciful story and how Miss Lotta Scales underwent her transformation from a dragon into a caring librarian.

2. On the second reading, tell the students that they are going to complete a Five Senses Box. Complete a box like the example below as you read.

3. Then discuss how all these factors help develop the mood or tone of the story. How would the students describe the tone? Fanciful? Serious? Humorous? A combination?

Describe what you could see:
Describe what you could hear:
Describe what you could smell:
Describe what you could touch:
Describe what you could taste:

Related books

Stewart, Sarah. *The Library.* Illustrated by David Small. New York: Farrar, Straus & Giroux, 1995.

Thompson, Colin. *How to Live Forever.* New York: Alfred A. Knopf, 1995.

From: Bridges to Reading, Grades K-3: Teaching Reading Skills with Children's Literature. © 1999 Suzanne I. Barchers. Teacher Ideas Press (800) 237-6124.

From: Bridges to Reading, Grades K-3: Teaching Reading Skills with Children's Literature. © 1999 Suzanne I. Barchers. Teacher Ideas Press (800) 237-6124.

Mandel, Peter. *Red Cat White Cat.* Illustrated by Clare Mackie. New York: Henry Holt, 1994.

Grade levels: K–1.

Every cat in this book has an opposite. The red cat is paired with a white cat. The day cat is paired with a night cat. Each pair of cats is portrayed in humorous and simple terms. This is a perfect introduction to the meaning of opposites.

Activities

1. Ask how many students have a cat for a pet. Make a chart such as the example below that compares their features. Let the students contribute suggestions for comparisons.

2. Read the book aloud. Discuss the opposites presented in the book. Can the students categorize the cats further? Do they have any opposites among their cats?

3. If preferred, repeat the process with dogs. How would the pairs of opposites change with dogs? How would they stay the same? Create a new book that describes dogs.

4. What pairs of animals seem to be opposites? For example, an elephant and a mouse are often paired together. Other opposites might be birds and worms, cats and dogs, cats and rats. What makes them opposites?

5. Look around the classroom. What examples of opposites can the students find? Consider colors, shapes, clothing, and other criteria.

Cat's name	Cat's color	Cat's size	Inside or outside cat	Cat's age	Hair length

Opposites

Related books

Jeram, Anita. *Contrary Mary.* Cambridge, Mass.: Candlewick Press, 1995.

Leedy, Loreen. *Big, Small, Short, Tall.* New York: Holiday House, 1987.

McMillan, Bruce. *Becca Backward, Becca Frontward: A Book of Concept Pairs.* New York: Lothrop, Lee and Shepard, 1986.

Root, Phyllis. *Contrary Bear.* New York: HarperCollins, 1996.

Schroeder, Pamela J. P., and Jean M. Donisch. *What's the Big Idea? Opposites.* Vero Beach, Fla.: Rourke, 1996.

From: Bridges to Reading, Grades K-3: Teaching Reading Skills with Children's Literature. © 1999 Suzanne I. Barchers. Teacher Ideas Press (800) 237-6124.

Jeram, Anita. *Contrary Mary.* Cambridge, Mass.: Candlewick Press, 1995.

Grade levels: 2–3.

Mary wakes up feeling contrary. She puts her clothes on wrong, requests roast potatoes and gravy for breakfast, rides her bicycle backwards, and walks on her hands. Her mother cooperates with Mary's contrariness, right up until bedtime.

Activities

1. Before reading the story, ask the students if they have ever heard of the phrase "getting up on the wrong side of the bed." Discuss how that means that you may feel out of sorts all day long.

2. Read *Contrary Mary* aloud. Ask the students if they have ever wanted to do things the exact opposite of what they normally do. Read the story again and have the students identify all the things Mary does that are the opposite of what one expects. Make a list such as the one shown below.

3. Plan an opposites day at school. Have the students brainstorm what might occur. For example, they might wear slippers and pajamas to school, have reading and other subjects at different times, teach the classes while the teacher studies, and eat breakfast instead of lunch. Let them think of many possibilities and then choose those opposite behaviors that will be acceptable.

What Mary Did	What Mary Should Have Done
Put her cap on backward.	Put her cap on forward.
Put her shoes on the wrong feet.	Put her shoes on the right feet.
Told her mother she wasn't awake.	Told her mother she was awake.

From: Bridges to Reading, Grades K-3: Teaching Reading Skills with Children's Literature. © 1999 Suzanne I. Barchers. Teacher Ideas Press (800) 237-6124.

Opposites

Related books

Leedy, Loreen. *Big, Small, Short, Tall.* New York: Holiday House, 1987.

Mandel, Peter. *Red Cat White Cat.* Illustrated by Clare Mackie. New York: Holt, 1994.

McMillan, Bruce. *Becca Backward, Becca Frontward: A Book of Concept Pairs.* New York: Lothrop, Lee and Shepard, 1986.

Root, Phyllis. *Contrary Bear.* New York: HarperCollins, 1996.

Schroeder, Pamela J. P., and Jean M. Donisch. *What's the Big Idea? Opposites.* Vero Beach, Fla.: Rourke, 1996.

From: Bridges to Reading, Grades K-3: Teaching Reading Skills with Children's Literature. © 1999 Suzanne I. Barchers. Teacher Ideas Press (800) 237-6124.

From: Bridges to Reading, Grades K–3: Teaching Reading Skills with Children's Literature. © 1999 Suzanne I. Barchers. Teacher Ideas Press (800) 237-6124.

 Van Laan, Nancy. *Possum Come a-Knocking.* Illustrated by George Booth. New York: Alfred A. Knopf, 1990.

Grade levels: K–1.

In this rhythmic and repetitive book, a possum comes knocking at the door. The dog, cat, and child hear it, but everyone else ignores the possum's repeated knocking. Finally, the animals and child put up such a fuss that the others check out the front porch—but the possum has hidden.

Activities

1. Practice reading this book aloud beforehand. The rhythms are strong and, with practice, the reading can be very entertaining.

2. Start by asking if the students know what a possum is. Show a picture of one, if available.

3. Read the story aloud to the class. On the second reading, invite the students to join in with the repetitive lines.

4. Obtain multiple copies of the book through interlibrary loan or by purchasing them. Have the students take on the different roles: Sis, Brother, Granny, Pa, and Pappy. The teacher should consider taking on the role of the child, who serves as the narrator, for the first time. Give the students an opportunity to practice their parts.

5. Practice reading through the story with the students reading the various roles. Then, share the story with the rest of the class or with another class. Consider preparing several stories or poems for sharing and having a session of choral reading.

Related books

Hopkins, Lee Bennett. *Good Rhymes, Good Times.* Illustrated by Frané Lessac. New York: HarperCollins, 1995.

Malone, Peter. *Star Shapes.* San Francisco: Chronicle, 1997.

Prelutsky, Jack. *The Dragons Are Singing Tonight.* Illustrated by Peter Sís. New York: Morrow, 1993.

———. *Tyrannosaurus Was a Beast.* Illustrated by Arnold Lobel. New York: Greenwillow, 1988.

Prelutsky, Jack. *The Dragons Are Singing Tonight.* Illustrated by Peter Sís. New York: Morrow, 1993.

Grade levels: 2–3.

In this collection of poems, Prelutsky pays homage to the legendary dragon. Every child who has fantasized about dragons will enjoy the poems such as "I'm an Amiable Dragon," "I Am Waiting Waiting Waiting," and "I Wish I Had a Dragon." Students will enjoy the humor of a dragon losing its fire in a thunderstorm. The varying lengths and difficulty levels of the vocabulary make this book especially useful for classroom use.

Activities

1. Read the poems aloud, giving students time to enjoy the illustrations.

2. Allow the students to choose a poem from the book, giving them time to copy it onto paper. Then give the students time to practice reading their poem aloud. Have the students work with partners, encouraging them to critique delivery and pronunciation to ensure that listeners will be able to understand the words.

3. Give students the option of creating their own dragon poems. Allow ample time to rehearse their original poems.

4. Declare a dragon day. Have the students create simple props or costumes to enhance their presentations. Have the students read aloud their poems to the others in the class.

5. Celebrate by having a dragon party. Serve dragon-hot foods, such as chili, chips and salsa, and red-hots.

Related books

Cassedy, Sylvia. *Zoomrimes: Poems About Things That Go.* Illustrated by Michele Chessare. New York: HarperCollins, 1993.

Otten, Charlotte F. *January Rides the Wind: A Book of Months.* Illustrated by Todd L. W. Doney. New York: Morrow, 1997.

Prelutsky, Jack. *Tyrannosaurus Was a Beast.* Illustrated by Arnold Lobel. New York: Greenwillow, 1988.

From: Bridges to Reading, Grades K–3: Teaching Reading Skills with Children's Literature. © 1999 Suzanne I. Barchers. Teacher Ideas Press (800) 237-6124.

From: Bridges to Reading, Grades K–3: Teaching Reading Skills with Children's Literature. © 1999 Suzanne I. Barchers. Teacher Ideas Press (800) 237-6124.

Tarsky, Sue. *The Busy Building Book.* Illustrated by Alex Ayliffe. New York: G. P. Putnam's Sons, 1997.

Grade levels: K–1.

The construction site is carefully prepared before construction actually begins. After excavation, the foundation is prepared. Next, scaffolding allows workers to stand or sit as the skeleton goes up. The floors are added, and the outside is finished. Then a variety of new workers, such as plumbers and electricians, prepare the inside. Finally, moving day arrives, the building is cleaned, and the owners welcome people at opening day ceremonies.

Activities

1. Read the book aloud to the students. You may need to allow two or more sessions to do this because of the many labels throughout the book.

2. After finishing the book, return to the beginning and read just the text. When finished with the second reading, ask the students to help you list the 12 main steps to building a building. For example, the first three steps might be paraphrased as follows:

   1. The construction site is prepared.
   2. The workers dig a hole.
   3. The foundation is laid.

3. When finished, review the book again. Check the text against the list of steps. Did the students remember everything?

4. Give each student three pieces of drawing paper. Have them fold each piece in half twice, giving them 12 squares to work in. Have them copy the 12 steps of the building into the squares. Then have them illustrate the steps of creating the building. If time is limited, divide the students into groups of three and have the groups complete the drawings.

Related books

Bare, Colleen Stanley. *This Is a House.* New York: Dutton, 1992.

Burton, Virginia Lee. *Mike Mulligan and His Steam Shovel.* Boston: Houghton Mifflin, 1939.

Gibbons, Gail. *How a House Is Built.* New York: Holiday House, 1990.

Paraphrasing

Gibbons, Gail. *Planet Earth/Inside Out.* New York: Morrow, 1995.

Grade levels: 2–3.

This informational book describes how scientists think the earth was formed, how *Pangaea* (the single landmass) broke apart, and how the oceans were formed. The inside of the earth is described, with diagrams showing the core, mantle, crust, and other layers. Earthquakes, volcanoes, tsunamis, and glaciers are also described. The book concludes with a description of Earth's rocks.

Activities

1. Before reading the book, draw a large circle on the board. Tell the students that the circle represents something very important in their lives. Let them guess, giving them clues until they guess that it represents Earth.

2. Ask the students to tell you everything they know about the earth. Write the facts in or around the circle. Save the information.

3. Read the book aloud, splitting it into sections if necessary. While reading it, circle any information that was written on the board that is discussed in the book.

4. Before reading the book a second time, tell the students that they will be writing down three new facts that they learn from listening to the book. Model note-taking by reading aloud the first page. Discuss how you could write down the phrase *right environment* for your notes, returning to it later to write a complete sentence. Then create the sentence that the note inspired.

5. Let the students sit at their desks with paper and pencil so that they can write while you read. After they write their sentences, discuss how paraphrasing is a valuable research skill that they can use the rest of their lives.

Related books

Caduto, Michael J. *Earth Tales from Around the World.* Illustrated by Adelaide Murphy Tyrol. Golden, Colo.: Fulcrum, 1997.

Lauber, Patricia. *How We Learned the Earth Is Round.* Illustrated by Megan Lloyd. New York: Thomas Y. Crowell, 1990.

———. *You're Aboard Spaceship Earth.* Illustrated by Holly Keller. New York: Harper-Collins, 1996.

Luenn, Nancy. *Mother Earth.* Illustrated by Neil Waldman. New York: Atheneum, 1992.

From: Bridges to Reading, Grades K–3: Teaching Reading Skills with Children's Literature. © 1999 Suzanne I. Barchers. Teacher Ideas Press (800) 237-6124.

Giganti, Paul. *Each Orange Had 8 Slices.* Illustrated by Donald Crews. New York: Trumpet, 1992.

Grade levels: K–1.

The narrator describes all the things seen en route to various locations. For example, three waddling ducks, plus four baby ducks for each waddling duck, are seen on the way to the zoo. This interactive counting book allows the students to respond to questions about the number of items seen on each double-page spread.

Activities

1. Begin to help students understand adjectives by talking about all the things we see around us and that we often describe when talking about them. Discuss how, in this book, the narrator sees many things and loves to count them. Read the book aloud, allowing students to respond to the questions.

2. Read the book aloud again. This time, stop with each page or set of pages to write on the board the things that are seen. For example, create this list for the first page:

   > 3 red flowers
   > 6 pretty petals
   > 2 tiny black bugs

3. After writing each list on the board, ask the students to decide which words describe the objects. Use colored chalk to underline the adjectives. Leave the lists on the board for now.

4. At another time, return to the lists and tell the students you are going to make a word bank of only adjectives. Have them identify all the underlined words and list them under the heading of *Adjectives.*

Related books

Boynton, Sandra. *A is for Angry: An Animal and Adjective Alphabet.* New York: Workman, 1983, 1987.

Hard, Charlotte. *One Green Island.* Cambridge, Mass.: Candlewick Press, 1995.

Lottridge, Celia Barker. *One Watermelon Seed.* Illustrated by Karen Patkau. Toronto: Oxford University Press, 1986.

From: Bridges to Reading, Grades K–3: Teaching Reading Skills with Children's Literature. © 1999 Suzanne I. Barchers. Teacher Ideas Press (800) 237-6124.

Parts of Speech: Adjectives

 Barton, Byron. *The Wee Little Woman.* New York: HarperCollins, 1995.

Grade levels: 2–3.

Everything the Wee Little Woman owns is small. Her house, cat, cow, stool, and pail—even her voice—are tiny. But when the wee little cat laps up all her milk, she uses her *loudest* wee little voice to make it scat. Soon she misses her wee little cat, welcoming it with a wee little bowl of milk when it returns.

Activities

1. Before reading the book, ask the students to think of small things, such as mosquitoes, kittens, buttons, and dust specks. Then have them think of all the words that mean "little." Write them on the board. Tell them that they are going to listen to a story about many little things.

2. After reading the book aloud, ask the students what two words in the book indicated size (*wee, little*). Tell the students that when you read the book again they should count the number of times the author uses *wee, little* (37).

3. Explain that words that describe something are called adjectives. Read the story again and ask the students to identify other adjectives (*loudest, wee, long, very hungry*). Talk about the nouns that the words describe.

4. Ask the students to think of another pair of adjectives that describe the nouns in the book (*teeny tiny, itty bitty*). Read the story again, using the new adjectives.

5. Ask the students to think of another pair of adjectives that would be opposites, such as *big, huge*. Read the story again, substituting the opposites. How does doing so affect the story?

Related books

Boynton, Sandra. *A is for Angry: An Animal and Adjective Alphabet.* New York: Workman, 1983, 1987.

Calmenson, Stephanie. *The Teeny Tiny Teacher.* Illustrated by Denis Roche. New York: Scholastic, 1998.

Heller, Ruth. *Many Luscious Lollipops: A Book About Adjectives.* New York: Putnam, 1989.

Winters, Kay. *The Teeny Tiny Ghost.* Illustrated by Lynn Munsinger. New York: HarperCollins, 1997.

From: Bridges to Reading, Grades K-3: Teaching Reading Skills with Children's Literature. © 1999 Suzanne I. Barchers. Teacher Ideas Press (800) 237-6124.

From: Bridges to Reading, Grades K–3: Teaching Reading Skills with Children's Literature. © 1999 Suzanne I. Barchers. Teacher Ideas Press (800) 237-6124.

 Gustafson, Scott. *Animal Orchestra.* Shelton, Conn.: The Greenwich Workshop, 1995.

Grade levels: 2–3.

This counting book simply provides directions for creating an animal orchestra. Beginning with 1 conductor, you add 2 double basses, and then you add more animals playing instruments until you include 10 flutes. Finally, you have all the makings of one fine animal orchestra.

Activities

1. Discuss how adverbs are words that tell how, how often, when, and where. Generate a list of adverbs by brainstorming words that give such information. If the students are mature, introduce Ruth Heller's *Up, Up and Away: A Book About Adverbs* (see the "Related books" section below). Read enough information from it so that students understand how adverbs function.

2. Read *Animal Orchestra* aloud. Then explain to the students that they are going to add verbs and adverbs to each orchestra direction in the book. Brainstorm a number of possibilities for each one. For example, *1 conductor* could become *1 conductor conducting wildly.* The flutists could be tooting tunefully.

3. After discussing a variety of ideas, let the students create their own versions of the counting book, adding their choice of verbs and adverbs.

4. For an advanced challenge, refer to the list of animal performers in the back of the book. Can the small groups of students add verbs and adverbs that fit the individual animals?

Related books

Heller, Ruth. *Up, Up and Away: A Book About Adverbs.* New York: Putnam, 1991.

Murphy, Stuart J. *The Best Bug Parade.* Illustrated by Holly Keller. New York: Harper-Collins, 1996.

Risso, Mario. *Safari Grammar.* Lincolnwood, Ill.: NTC Publishing Group, 1989.

Sloat, Teri. *From One to One Hundred.* New York: Penguin, 1991.

Grade levels: K–1.

Each page of this nearly wordless counting book features a full-color illustration. Below the illustration is a number and a variety of small illustrations. The number indicates that the reader can find that number of those particular items in the picture above. The numbers covered include 1 through 10, plus 20, 30, 40, 50, 60, 70, 80, 90, and 100.

Activities

1. Each of the small illustrations can be identified as a noun, the name of a person, place, or thing. First introduce the book as a counting book, sharing the illustrations and numbers.

2. Next, discuss the meaning of the word *noun*. Return to the book and examine it for pictures of nouns. For example, on the first page, the indicated nouns include *castle*, *marshmallow*, *dragon*, *tree*, and *apple*. Challenge the students to find additional nouns: *grass*, *fire*, *knothole*, *drawbridge*, and *moat*, among others. Write the nouns on the board.

3. Have pairs or small groups of students make word splashes of related nouns. A word splash is made by simply arranging related words on a piece of paper in random order with the central concept in the middle of the page. For example, a word splash about rain might include the following words: *puddle*, *umbrella*, *clouds*, *rainbow*, and *raindrops*.

4. Place the same selection of numbers as found in the book in a can or box. Have each pair or group draw a number. Have the students take each word splash and turn it into an illustration similar to those in the book. Compile the results in a book.

Related books

Merriam, Eve. *12 Ways to Get to 11.* Illustrated by Bernie Karlin. New York: Trumpet, 1992.

O'Donnell, Elizabeth Lee. *Winter Visitors.* Illustrated by Carol Schwartz. New York: Morrow, 1997.

Pittman, Helena Clare. *Counting Jennie.* Minneapolis, Minn.: Carolrhoda Books, 1994.

From: Bridges to Reading, Grades K-3: Teaching Reading Skills with Children's Literature. © 1999 Suzanne I. Barchers. Teacher Ideas Press (800) 237-6124.

Merriam, Eve. *12 Ways to Get to 11*. Illustrated by Bernie Karlin. New York: Trumpet, 1992.

Grade levels: 2–3.

This colorful counting book begins by counting from 1 to 10, skipping 11, and continuing to 12. It asks the question "Where is 11?" and proceeds to show 12 ways to get 11. For example, picking up nine pinecones and two acorns adds up to 11. Six peanut shells and five pieces of popcorn total 11 items at the circus. The students can learn about nouns while reinforcing math skills.

Activities

1. Read the book aloud. Then discuss how a variety of things were used to make 11. Discuss the use of addition to get the combinations that make 11. Then, explain that names of things are called nouns.

2. Tell the students that you are going to read the book again. This time they should raise their hands every time you read a noun. Write the nouns on the board. Create a word bank of the nouns.

3. Next, create a new book that shows other number combinations. For example, students could work in pairs or small groups to write and illustrate *11 Ways to Get to 10*. Have the students write all the nouns in a distinctive color to reinforce the meaning of nouns.

4. For a variation, create a spin-off of the book, using subtraction. For example, the book could start with 12 candles. One burns down, leaving 11. The next page could have 13 ice cream cones. Two melt, leaving 11 ice cream cones.

Related books

Heller, Ruth. *Merry-Go-Round: A Book About Nouns*. New York: Putnam and Grosset, 1990.

O'Donnell, Elizabeth Lee. *Winter Visitors*. Illustrated by Carol Schwartz. New York: Morrow, 1997.

Pittman, Helena Clare. *Counting Jennie*. Minneapolis, Minn.: Carolrhoda Books, 1994.

Sloat, Teri. *From One to One Hundred*. New York: Penguin, 1991.

From: Bridges to Reading, Grades K-3: Teaching Reading Skills with Children's Literature. © 1999 Suzanne I. Barchers. Teacher Ideas Press (800) 237-6124.

Parts of Speech: Prepositions

Hoban, Tana. *All About Where.* New York: Greenwillow, 1991.

Grade levels: 2–3.

This innovative book lists 15 prepositions in the margins of the first and last pages. Between these pages, the reader can study a variety of color photographs and find examples of the prepositions: *above, on, behind, under, out, against, across,* and others.

Activities

1. Begin by sharing the pictures and asking questions about them. For example, in the first picture, ask where the jump ropes are. (Over the girl's head; under the other girl's feet.) Continue through the pictures, talking about where the people or things are.

2. Introduce the word *preposition.* Explain that prepositions are the words that show a relationship and that they are always in a prepositional phrase. Return to the book and review the phrases you generated through the questioning. Write a variety of them on the board.

3. Ask the students if they can think of other prepositions. It helps to think of opposites: *after/before; off/on; within/without.* List as many prepositions as possible.

4. Have the students make their own preposition book. Have them work in small groups and use magazines to find pictures to illustrate the relationships. Label the pictures with appropriate prepositional phrases explaining the relationship.

5. Create an obstacle course in the classroom or playground. Label the course. For example, on a table, place a sign that says, "Go *under* the table." Have a preposition day when you work at writing down every preposition used throughout the day.

Related books

Aardema, Verna. *This for That.* Illustrated by Victoria Chess. New York: Penguin, 1997.

Crebbin, June. *Into the Castle.* Illustrated by John Bendall-Brunello. Cambridge, Mass.: Candlewick Press, 1996.

Heiligman, Deborah. *On the Move.* Illustrated by Lizzy Rockwell. New York: HarperCollins, 1996.

Heller, Ruth. *Behind the Mask.* New York: Grosset & Dunlap, 1995.

Hoban, Tana. *Over, Under and Through.* New York: Macmillan, 1973.

Miller, Margaret. *Where Does It Go?* New York: Morrow, 1998.

From: Bridges to Reading, Grades K–3: Teaching Reading Skills with Children's Literature. © 1999 Suzanne I. Barchers. Teacher Ideas Press (800) 237-6124.

Newcome, Zita. *Toddlerobics.* Cambridge, Mass.: Candlewick Press, 1996.
Grade levels: 2–3.

When toddler gym begins, eight toddlers begin to flap their arms, lift their feet, stretch up high, bend down low, lift their rattles, clap, stamp, nod, and dance. The fun continues as they play actively together until it's time to get ready to go home. This entertaining book will encourage listeners to participate in the fun! Note: One illustration shows a toddler's partially bare bottom. If this is problematic, use an alternate book, Eric Carle's *From Head to Toe* (see "Related books" section below).

Activities

1. Read the book aloud. Then talk about the words that describe the action: *flap*, *lift*, *stretch*, *bend*. Tell the students that these action words are called verbs. Read the story again, telling the students to raise their hands every time they hear an action word. List them on the board.

2. Together, read the words listed on the board through the word *dance*. Then tell the students that they are going to act out the words as you read them. Do this as a group.

3. Then discuss the verbs that require the rest of the phrase or sentence to be clear. Act out those actions as space and time allow.

4. Look through the pictures and have students identify actions that were not listed. For example, on the last double-page spread, you can see children dress, pinch, wave, and kiss. Talk about the verbs.

5. Ask the students to think of other actions that they could do. First think of active things, such as jump, run, and leap. To bring closure, challenge them to think of quiet things: yawn, smile, shrug, wink, and breathe.

Related books

Carle, Eric. *From Head to Toe.* New York: HarperCollins, 1997.

Gomi, Taro. *Seeing, Saying, Doing, Playing: A Big Book of Action Words.* San Francisco: Chronicle, 1991.

Heller, Ruth. *Kites Sail High: A Book About Verbs.* New York: Grosset & Dunlap, 1988.

Rotner, Shelley. *Action Alphabet.* New York: Simon & Schuster, 1996.

Schneider, R. M. *Add It Dip It Fix It: A Book of Verbs.* Boston: Houghton Mifflin, 1995.

Shaw, Nancy. *Sheep on a Ship.* Illustrated by Margot Apple. Boston: Houghton Mifflin, 1989.

———. *Sheep Out to Eat.* Illustrated by Margot Apple. Boston: Houghton Mifflin, 1992.

From: Bridges to Reading, Grades K–3: Teaching Reading Skills with Children's Literature. © 1999 Suzanne I. Barchers. Teacher Ideas Press (800) 237-6124.

Phrases/Sentences

Perry, Sarah. *If . . . .* Malibu, Calif.: J. Paul Getty Museum/Children's Library Press, 1995.

Grade levels: 2–3.

The fanciful illustrations and simple sentences present a series of premises, such as what cats would look like if they could fly. Some of the illustrations are quite arresting, such as the ones showing mice as hair, toes as teeth, and caterpillars as toothpaste. Students will be fascinated with this delightful book.

Activities

1. Read the book aloud, allowing ample time for students to study the illustrations.

2. On the second reading, discuss how each page includes only a phrase. Discuss the author's use of ellipses and how the result is to leave the reader's thoughts somewhat suspended.

3. Read through the book again slowly. Ask the students to complete the rest of each sentence. For example, the first one might read as follows: *If cats could fly, they would have wings.* Continue through the book, accepting all possible variations on the sentences and recording them on chart paper or on the board.

4. Follow the book's advice at the end and work together as a class to create a new version of it. Brainstorm lots of possibilities: *if anteaters were pets . . . ; if cars traveled on rails . . . ; if dogs loved cats. . . .* Let the students then work independently or in small groups to create their own examples. Have the students illustrate the pages and compile them in a class book.

Related books

Diviny, Sean. *Snow Inside the House.* Illustrated by Joe Rocco. New York: HarperCollins, 1998.

Hillman, Ben. *That Pesky Toaster.* New York: Hyperion, 1995.

Longfellow, Layne. *Imaginary Menagerie.* Illustrated by Woodleigh Marx Hubbard. San Francisco: Chronicle, 1997.

Wood, Audrey. *Bright and Early Thursday Evening: A Tangled Tale.* Illustrated by Don Wood. San Diego, Calif.: Harcourt Brace, 1996.

From: Bridges to Reading, Grades K–3: Teaching Reading Skills with Children's Literature. © 1999 Suzanne I. Barchers. Teacher Ideas Press (800) 237-6124.

From: Bridges to Reading, Grades K–3: Teaching Reading Skills with Children's Literature. © 1999 Suzanne I. Barchers. Teacher Ideas Press (800) 237-6124.

Hutchins, Pat. *The Doorbell Rang.* New York: Greenwillow, 1986.

Grade levels: K–1.

Ma has made a dozen cookies, plenty for Victoria and Sam to share. But then the doorbell rings and two more children arrive. The four children decide to divide the cookies four ways, but then the doorbell rings again. This continues until there are a dozen children and the doorbell rings once more . . . signaling the arrival of Victoria and Sam's grandmother with more cookies!

Activities

1. Begin reading the book. Stop when the doorbell rings and ask the students what they think will happen next. Continue reading and stopping every time the doorbell rings. Each time, the students predict what will happen next. Discuss other endings that the author might have chosen for the story. Can the students come up with an ending as satisfying as this one?

2. Reread the book. Have the students work out the number of cookies each person will have until the doorbell rings. Use cookies to demonstrate the math if necessary.

3. Have the students act out the story, with 12 students taking the parts of the children and 2 students taking the adult roles. Have the rest of the class act as the audience. Then rotate the roles so everyone has a chance to perform.

4. Have the students work in small groups to create a new ending to the story. Perhaps more children will arrive, the grandmother will arrive with a gallon of milk, or the mail carrier will appear at the door. Have the students act out the new version, stopping so that the audience can predict what will happen at the end.

Related books

Axelrod, Amy. *Pigs in the Pantry.* Illustrated by Sharon McGinley-Nally. New York: Simon & Schuster, 1997.

Christelow, Eileen. *Don't Wake Up Mama!* New York: Trumpet, 1992.

Day, Alexandra. *Frank and Ernest.* New York: Scholastic, 1988.

Pinczes, Elinor. *One Hundred Hungry Ants.* Illustrated by Bonnie MacKain. New York: Scholastic, 1993.

MacDonald, Margaret Read. *Pickin' Peas.* Illustrated by Pat Cummings. New York: HarperCollins, 1998.

Grade levels: 2–3.

When Little Girl went into her garden to pick her peas, she discovered a pesky rabbit. He was hopping along, eating and singing. She caught the rabbit and took him into her house. But the rabbit convinced her to let him entertain her with his dancing. When she let him out, he danced right out the window. The very next morning he was back in the garden, picking peas and singing.

Activities

1. Read the book up to the point where Little Girl realizes there is a rabbit in her garden. Stop and ask the students what they think will happen next. Continue with the story, stopping at appropriate intervals to allow the students to predict the next event. Did they predict that the rabbit was tricking Little Girl when he said he could dance and entertain her?

2. Read the story again and let the students join you when the rabbit sings. Teach them the song or create your own song, as discussed at the end of the book.

3. Create a story map that describes the events in the story. Use the form on page 103 or adapt the process as necessary.

Related books

Cushman, Doug. *Mouse and Mole and the Year-Round Garden.* New York: Trumpet, 1994.

Lerner, Carol. *My Backyard Garden.* New York: Morrow, 1998.

Lottridge, Celia Barker. *One Watermelon Seed.* Illustrated by Karen Patkau. Toronto: Oxford University Press, 1986.

Stevens, Janet. *Tops and Bottoms.* San Diego, Calif.: Harcourt Brace, 1995.

From: Bridges to Reading, Grades K–3: Teaching Reading Skills with Children's Literature. © 1999 Suzanne I. Barchers. Teacher Ideas Press (800) 237-6124.

Story Map

Title of Book:	
Setting(s):	
Character(s):	
Problem(s):	
Events: 1.	
2.	
3.	
4.	
5.	
Resolution:	

From: Bridges to Reading, Grades K-3: Teaching Reading Skills with Children's Literature. © 1999 Suzanne I. Barchers. Teacher Ideas Press (800) 237-6124.

Rebuses

Neitzel, Shirley. *The Bag I'm Taking to Grandma's.* Illustrated by Nancy Winslow Parker. New York: Greenwillow, 1995.

Grade levels: K–1.

In this cumulative story, a young boy plans what he will take in his bag to his grandma's: a mitt, his cars, a space shuttle and crew, animals, a bunny, a pillow, a book, and a flashlight. The bag is so heavy that his mother insists he remove some of the items. He removes them, but by the time his mother brings necessary items, such as clothes, he has his bag filled with toys again.

Activities

1. Begin by asking the students what they take when they go on an overnight to their grandparents', another relative's, or a friend's house. List these items on the board.

2. Read the book aloud, pointing out the use of rebuses in place of a number of the words. Tell the students that the use of rebuses will help them be able to read the book.

3. Reread the book, inviting the students to read the story with you. They should be able to read most of the text easily because of the repetition and use of rebuses.

4. Tell the students that they are going to create a new version of the story using rebuses. Give them the following starting sentences and have them add the pictures in the blanks.

Have them repeat the second sentence as many times as they want to, putting a picture in the blank.

Here is the bag I'm taking to _____.

Here is the _____ that I'll pack in the bag that I'm taking to Grandma's.

Related books

Martin, Pat, Joanne Kelly, and Kay Grabow. *Rebuses for Readers.* Englewood, Colo.: Teacher Ideas Press, 1992.

Morris, Ann. *The Cinderella Rebus Book.* Illustrated by Ljiljana Rylands. New York: Orchard, 1989.

From: Bridges to Reading, Grades K-3: Teaching Reading Skills with Children's Literature. © 1999 Suzanne I. Barchers. Teacher Ideas Press (800) 237-6124.

From: Bridges to Reading, Grades K-3: Teaching Reading Skills with Children's Literature. © 1999 Suzanne I. Barchers. Teacher Ideas Press (800) 237-6124.

Morris, Ann. *The Cinderella Rebus Book.* Illustrated by Ljiljana Rylands. New York: Orchard, 1989.

Grade levels: 2–3.

This retelling of the traditional story relies on the use of 75 rebuses for a wide variety of words or parts of words. The reading becomes more entertaining because of the rebuses but also more challenging. A rebus dictionary at the end of the story provides help if a rebus is not easily understood.

Activities

1. Ask the students if they remember the story of Cinderella. Ask them to identify some of the key people, places, animals, and items that make up the story. List them on the board. Then ask the students how they could illustrate some of them.

2. Share the book, explaining that the book uses rebuses, or small illustrations, in place of many words. Before reading the text, show the pictures and ask the students if they can guess what the pictures represent. Read the text and decide if their predictions were accurate.

3. Use the rebus dictionary at the end of the book to confirm any rebuses in the text that are unclear. Discuss how sometimes pictures are used in place of parts of words.

4. If possible, share a variety of the rebus puzzles from *Rebuses for Readers* (see the "Related books" section below).

5. Encourage the students to create their own stories using rebus puzzles. The stories can be much shorter than Morris's. If you have access to *Rebuses for Readers,* let the students create puzzles that challenge their classmates.

Related books

Martin, Pat, Joanne Kelly, and Kay Grabow. *Rebuses for Readers.* Englewood, Colo.: Teacher Ideas Press, 1992.

Neitzel, Shirley. *The Bag I'm Taking to Grandma's.* Illustrated by Nancy Winslow Parker. New York: Greenwillow, 1995.

105

Scieszka, Jon. *The Book That Jack Wrote.* Illustrated by Daniel Adel. New York: Viking, 1994.

Grade levels: K–1.

In this cumulative rhyme, Jack writes a book. He puts in a picture, a rat falls in the picture, a cat eats the rat, a dog chases the cat, a cow flies over the moon, a baby hums a tune, a pieman throws a pie, and so forth. Finally, the book squashes the last character, bringing the story full circle.

Activities

1. Ask the students if they have heard the poem "This Is the House That Jack Built." Explain that Jon Scieszka has created a new version of this story.

2. Read the book aloud, sharing the illustrations. On the second reading, ask the students to read along.

3. Discuss how the lines repeat as the story proceeds, a common structure for a story.

4. Review the books in the "Related books" list below. These present the same type of story structure with varying levels of difficulty.

5. Brainstorm other things that Jack might do in another version: bake a cake, drive a car, run a race, play a game. Choose a new scenario to develop as a class. Discuss events that could occur in the new version. Write the new version, incorporating rhyme and repetition as in Scieszka's version. Let students choose a portion of the book to illustrate.

Related books

Davol, Marguerite W. *The Heart of the Wood.* Illustrated by Sheila Hamanaka. New York: Simon & Schuster, 1992.

Lobel, Arnold. *The Rose in My Garden.* Illustrated by Anita Lobel. New York: Scholastic, 1984.

Neitzel, Shirley. *The Bag I'm Taking to Grandma's.* Illustrated by Nancy Winslow Parker. New York: Greenwillow, 1995.

Robart, Rose. *The Cake That Mack Ate.* Illustrated by Maryann Kovalski. Boston: Little, Brown, 1986.

From: Bridges to Reading, Grades K-3: Teaching Reading Skills with Children's Literature. © 1999 Suzanne I. Barchers. Teacher Ideas Press (800) 237-6124.

From: Bridges to Reading, Grades K–3: Teaching Reading Skills with Children's Literature. © 1999 Suzanne I. Barchers. Teacher Ideas Press (800) 237-6124.

Brown, Margaret Wise. *The Important Book.* Illustrated by Leonard Weisgard. New York: HarperCollins, 1949, 1977, 1990.

Grade levels: 2–3.

On each double-page spread, one reads about the important features of a variety of items: a spoon, a daisy, rain, grass, snow, an apple, the wind, the sky, a shoe, and you. Each discussion follows the same pattern, ending with a sentence that repeats the first sentence.

Activities

1. Choose a variety of items that are not discussed in the book and ask the students what is important about them, for example, what is important about the school, a tree, the library, a student, a teacher, a hat, boots.

2. Read the book aloud, inviting the students to repeat the last line with you.

3. Discuss how this book has a repetitive pattern. Each set of pages begins with a sentence that states the importance of something. Additional sentences follow, and the passage concludes with the repetition of the first sentence. Write the pattern of the opening sentence on the board:

   The important thing about _____ is that you/it _____.

4. Return to the initial discussion of items and write about them in the same pattern as the book. Then have the students each choose something to write about using the same pattern.

5. Share all the writings the students have prepared. Then compile them into a collection for a classroom *Important Book.*

Related books

Archambault, John, and Bill Martin Jr. *A Beautiful Feast for a Big King Cat.* Illustrated by Bruce Degen. New York: HarperCollins, 1989.

Hennessy, B. G. *Jake Baked the Cake.* Illustrated by Mary Morgan. New York: Penguin, 1992.

Ivimey, John W. *Three Blind Mice.* Illustrated by Paul Galdone. New York: Trumpet, 1987.

Rhyme

Brown, Rick. *What Rhymes with Snake?* New York: Morrow, 1994.

Grade levels: K–1.

In this clever lift-flap book, a large picture is displayed, such as a hen. But when the flap over the *h* is lifted, a *p* appears. When the hen flap is lifted, the remaining portion of the beak transforms into the tip of a pen. Each set of words and pictures is cleverly illustrated, clearly showing the relationship between words and rhyming.

Activities

1. Read the book aloud, asking the students to predict the rhyming word and picture under each flap. Share the pictures. Then see if the students can think of other words that might work as rhymes.

2. Keep a list of the words the students think of that could be the basis for rhymes. Then begin an additional set of pairs of words. Some easy words include *can* (fan, man, pan); *ship* (hip, trip, slip); *gate* (date, plate, skate). Consult a rhyming dictionary, such as Sue Young's *The Scholastic Rhyming Dictionary* (see the "Related books" section below) for additional ideas.

3. Have the students create individual pages for a class lift-flap book. Write down the words for them if necessary. Use the same construction design as that in Brown's book. Reinforce the joints for the flaps with heavy package sealing tape. Compile the students' pages into a book. If possible, create a second copy for the library, or have students create a copy of their page to take home.

4. Begin a word wall or card file of word families that rhyme. Let the students use this source when creating rhyming poetry. Share many poems that rhyme and discuss the use of the words.

Related books

Janeczko, Paul B. *Poetry from A to Z: A Guide for Young Writers.* New York: Macmillan, 1994.

Lansky, Bruce. *Kids Pick the Funniest Poems.* Illustrated by Stephen Carpenter. Deephaven, Minn.: Meadowbrook Press, 1991.

Prelutsky, Jack. *The New Kid on the Block.* Illustrated by James Stevenson. New York: Scholastic, 1984.

Silverstein, Shel. *Where the Sidewalk Ends.* New York: Harper & Row, 1974.

Young, Sue. *The Scholastic Rhyming Dictionary.* New York: Scholastic, 1994.

From: Bridges to Reading, Grades K–3: Teaching Reading Skills with Children's Literature. © 1999 Suzanne I. Barchers. Teacher Ideas Press (800) 237-6124.

From: Bridges to Reading, Grades K–3: Teaching Reading Skills with Children's Literature. © 1999 Suzanne I. Barchers. Teacher Ideas Press (800) 237-6124.

Clements, Andrew. *Double Trouble in Walla Walla.* Illustrated by Salvatore Murdocca. Brookfield, Conn.: Millbrook Press, 1997.

Grade levels: 2–3.

In this zany story, Lulu disrupts her English class when she starts using a wealth of double words such as *higgledy-piggledy, tip-top,* and *mish-mash.* Then the teacher starts using words such as *flip-flop, chitter-chatter,* and *double-trouble.* Lulu and the teacher can't stop. They go to the principal and nurse, but it isn't until everyone says as many doubles as they can that they clear the air and everyone returns to normal (almost).

Activities

1. Read the book aloud. During the second reading, tell the students that they are to listen for all the double words. Have them call out the words and write them on the board. This will take a rather long time; as a result, this activity may need to be split into two time periods.

2. Refer to the list and decide which pairs of doubles are rhyming, which use alliteration, and which are repetitive. Sort out the list into categories, adding any other categories that make sense.

3. Discuss the uses of the word doubles. Do they seem to be overused? Or does the silly story make their use "okey-dokey."

4. Using a resource such as Sue Young's *The Scholastic Rhyming Dictionary* (see the "Related books" section below), try to identify other examples of double words.

5. Encourage the students to make up some short rhymes using some of the pairs. A good source of inspiration is that portion of the book toward the end where the characters offer a variety of examples.

Related books

Janeczko, Paul B. *Poetry from A to Z: A Guide for Young Writers.* New York: Macmillan, 1994.

Lansky, Bruce. *Kids Pick the Funniest Poems.* Illustrated by Stephen Carpenter. Deephaven, Minn.: Meadowbrook Press, 1991.

Young, Sue. *The Scholastic Rhyming Dictionary.* New York: Scholastic, 1994.

Andrews, Sylvia. *Rattlebone Rock.* Illustrated by Jennifer Plecas. New York: HarperCollins, 1995.

Grade levels: K–1.

Everyone remembers when the graveyard came alive. The skeletons danced, the ghosts swayed, the ghouls rapped and tapped, a banshee wailed, the goblins howled, and the witches stirred a brew. When the whole town began to shake, everyone rushed out to see what was happening. It looked like so much fun that everyone joined in, dancing to the Rattlebone Rock.

Activities

1. The words in this book almost dance off the page. Consider reading it around Halloween for a harmless look at ghosts, goblins, and other Halloween creatures.

2. Read the book aloud, emphasizing the rhythm. Share the examples of onomatopoeia, inviting the students to join in with the sound effects.

3. On the second reading, clap on the main beats of the rhyming lines. (In most cases, the stress occurs on the second word.) Invite the students to clap with you.

4. On the next reading, treat the book as a choral reading. Read two lines at a time, and have the students repeat them after you. Keep a strong beat. Students may join in on the third and fourth lines without needing the prompting at this point.

5. Discuss how the author used rhythm to make this an exciting book. Share other books with a strong rhythmic base (see the "Related books" section below) and invite the students to read along with you.

Related books

Baer, Gene. *THUMP, THUMP, Rat-a-Tat-Tat.* Illustrated by Lois Ehlert. New York: Harper, 1989, 1991.

Barner, Bob. *Dem Bones.* San Francisco: Chronicle, 1996.

La Prise, Larry, Charles P. Macak, and Taftt Baker. *The Hokey Pokey.* Illustrated by Sheila Hamanaka. New York: Simon & Schuster, 1997.

Van Laan, Nancy. *Possum Come a-Knocking.* Illustrated by George Booth. New York: Alfred A. Knopf, 1990.

From: Bridges to Reading, Grades K-3: Teaching Reading Skills with Children's Literature. © 1999 Suzanne I. Barchers; Teacher Ideas Press (800) 237-6124.

From: Bridges to Reading, Grades K-3: Teaching Reading Skills with Children's Literature. © 1999 Suzanne I. Barchers. Teacher Ideas Press (800) 237-6124.

 La Prise, Larry, Charles P. Macak, and Taftt Baker. *The Hokey Pokey.* Illustrated by Sheila Hamanaka. New York: Simon & Schuster, 1997.

Grade levels: 2–3.

This classic song and dance illustrate all the steps. From putting your right foot in and shaking it all about to putting your whole self in, the illustrations show an exuberant group of people and animals enjoying the song. This is an ideal book for a rainy day or when you need to energize the class.

Activities

1. Read the book aloud, showing the illustrations. Discuss the rhythm of the words and how the writers used repetition throughout the song.

2. After reading the book, have the students note how the key words, such as *right foot* and *left foot* are highlighted. Go through the book again, writing the highlighted words on the board to compile a list of the key steps: *right foot in, left foot in, right arm in,* and so forth.

3. If the students do not know the melody, teach the song, using the music presented at the beginning of the book if necessary.

4. Sing and dance the various verses. Emphasize keeping a strong rhythm throughout the dance.

5. If desired, create a drum, wood blocks (blocks covered with sandpaper), or other musical instruments to accompany the song. Repeat the game, with some of the students playing the instruments.

Related books

Barner, Bob. *Dem Bones.* San Francisco: Chronicle, 1996.

Oates, Eddie Herschel. *Making Music: 6 Instruments You Can Create.* Illustrated by Michael Koelsch. New York: HarperCollins, 1995.

Pearson, Tracey Campbell. *Old MacDonald Had a Farm.* New York: Dial, 1984.

Van Laan, Nancy. *Possum Come a-Knocking.* Illustrated by George Booth. New York: Alfred A. Knopf, 1990.

Sequence

 Zolotow, Charlotte. *When the Wind Stops.* Illustrated by Stefano Vitale. New York: HarperCollins, 1962, 1995.

Grade levels: K–1.

A little boy who has had a great day playing regrets seeing the day end. He asks his mother why the day must end, and she explains that day must end so that night can begin. He asks a series of questions, such as where the clouds go when they move across the sky, and his mother responds with an explanation of what happens next.

Activities

1. Read the book aloud. On the second reading, pause after each of the boy's questions, allowing the students to respond to what happens next. Elaborate on the natural order of time and the seasons. Then discuss what else might happen, accepting all reasonable answers.

2. Brainstorm other questions the boy might ask, such as where a river goes, where the full moon goes, where a flower goes when it dies. List the questions on the board. Then write all possible answers on the board as the next step in the sequence.

3. Give each student a large paper circle, approximately the size of a paper plate. Divide the circle into four equal portions. Have the students draw four scenes representing the four seasons. Discuss the sequence so that the order is correct.

Related books

George, Jean Craighead. *Dear Rebecca, Winter Is Here.* Illustrated by Loretta Krupinski. New York: HarperCollins, 1993.

Lewison, Wendy Cheyette. *Going to Sleep on the Farm.* Illustrated by Juan Wijngaard. New York: Dell, 1992.

Willard, Nancy. *Cracked Corn and Snow Ice Cream.* Illustrated by Jane Dyer. San Diego, Calif.: Harcourt Brace & Company, 1997.

From: Bridges to Reading, Grades K-3: Teaching Reading Skills with Children's Literature. © 1999 Suzanne I. Barchers. Teacher Ideas Press (800) 237-6124.

From: Bridges to Reading, Grades K–3: Teaching Reading Skills with Children's Literature. © 1999 Suzanne I. Barchers. Teacher Ideas Press (800) 237-6124.

Garay, Luis. *Pedrito's Day.* New York: Orchard, 1997.

Grade levels: 2–3.

Pedrito wants a bicycle and works hard to earn money to add to his secret savings. One day while at the market, his mother sends him to get change. He joins some boys playing soccer and loses the money. He confesses to his mother that he has lost the money, giving up some of his savings to replace it. His mother appreciates his honesty, and when Pedrito's father sends money from the north, a portion is added to his savings.

Activities

1. Read the story aloud. Discuss the key events in the story, beginning with Pedrito's father having gone north to work.

2. Ask the students to recall the key events in the story. Write them on the board. Reread the story and check that the sequence as they recalled the story is accurate. Add any omitted events or change the order as necessary.

3. Explain that authors often use a series of boxes, called a storyboard, to outline a story. Create a storyboard, such as that shown below, that shows the main events of *Pedrito's Day.* Then make up a simple story that describes what happens on the day Pedrito buys his bicycle. Write the key events in a storyboard, discussing the importance of the sequence of events.

Sample Storyboard

Related books

Bunting, Eve. *Market Day.* Illustrated by Holly Berry. New York: HarperCollins, 1996.

Bodnár, Judit Z. *A Wagonload of Fish.* Illustrated by Alexi Natchev. New York: Lothrop, Lee and Shepard, 1996.

Burningham, John. *The Shopping Basket.* Cambridge, Mass.: Candlewick Press, 1980, 1996.

Torres, Leyla. *Saturday Sancocho.* New York: Farrar, Straus & Giroux, 1995.

Summarization

 Paul, Ann Whitford. *Eight Hands Round: A Patchwork Alphabet.* Illustrated by Jeanette Winter. New York: HarperCollins, 1991.

Grade levels: 2–3.

A complete alphabet of quilt patterns is described through text and illustrations. For example, the blacksmith uses tongs to soften iron in fire before hammering it into shape on his anvil. The anvil pattern is reminiscent of the blacksmith's work. The varied patterns provide fascinating reading.

Activities

1. Bring in a quilt that has a distinctive pattern. Ask the students if they have any quilts at home. What pattern is on the quilt?

2. Read aloud the first description of the anvil pattern. Ask the students to help you write one sentence that describes this pattern. For example, the summarizing sentence might be:

   The anvil pattern looks like anvils next to each other and may have been thought up by a blacksmith or his wife.

3. Continue through the book, reading each section and having the students summarize the information into one sentence.

4. If possible, invite someone who quilts to visit your classroom. Ask him or her to show a variety of patterns and teach the students simple quilting.

5. Plan a quilt day with the students bringing in quilts to display. Research the patterns that are not included in the book and write a sentence summarizing the history of the pattern.

Related books

Musgrove, Margaret. *Ashanti to Zulu: African Traditions.* Illustrated by Leo and Diane Dillon. New York: Dial, 1976.

Pallotta, Jerry. *The Dinosaur Alphabet Book.* Illustrated by Ralph Masiello. New York: Trumpet, 1991.

———. *The Yucky Reptile Alphabet Book.* Illustrated by Ralph Masiello. New York: Trumpet, 1989.

From: Bridges to Reading, Grades K–3: Teaching Reading Skills with Children's Literature. © 1999 Suzanne I. Barchers. Teacher Ideas Press (800) 237-6124.

From: Bridges to Reading, Grades K–3: Teaching Reading Skills with Children's Literature. © 1999 Suzanne I. Barchers. Teacher Ideas Press (800) 237-6124.

Byars, Betsy. *The Golly Sisters Ride Again.* Illustrated by Sue Truesdell. New York: HarperCollins, 1994.

Grade levels: 2–3.

The Golly sisters love to sing and dance. In the first chapter of this easy book, Rose fears that the goat in the audience will bring bad luck. In the second chapter, the sisters deal with a talking rock. Next, they discuss who will be the princess in a play. Then they take a brief holiday. The book concludes with the sisters experiencing a storm.

Activities

1. Each chapter in this book can be easily summarized. Read aloud the first chapter, without reading the chapter title. Ask the students to tell you in their own words what the chapter was about. Then write a sentence describing the chapter on the board.

2. Ask the students to shorten the sentence even further to create a chapter title. Compare their title with the one in the book.

3. Continue reading the remaining chapters, repeating the process.

4. Divide the class into small groups. Give each group a chapter book with short chapters similar to those in *The Golly Sisters Ride Again.* (The "Related books" list below features several books that would be appropriate.) For each group, either obtain multiple copies or separate one copy of a book into chapters. Give each student in the group a chapter. Have each student read the chapter independently. Then have the students regroup and summarize each chapter in the order of the book. The students should each give enough information that the story line is understood, without giving detailed information.

Related books

Bottner, Barbara. *Bootsie Barker Ballerina.* Illustrated by G. Brian Karas. New York: HarperCollins, 1997.

Byars, Betsy. *The Seven Treasure Hunts.* New York: HarperCollins, 1991.

Calmenson, Stephanie, and Joanna Cole. *Rockin' Reptiles.* Illustrated by Lynn Munsinger. New York: Morrow, 1997.

Godwin, Laura. *Forest.* Illustrated by Stacey Schuett. New York: HarperCollins, 1998.

Himmelman, John. *The Animal Rescue Club.* New York: HarperCollins, 1998.

Levinson, Nancy Smiler. *Snowshoe Thompson.* Illustrated by Joan Sandin. New York: HarperCollins, 1992.

Text Structure: Cause and Effect

Lerner, Harriet, and Susan Goldhor. *What's So Terrible About Swallowing an Apple Seed?* Illustrated by Catharine O'Neil. New York: HarperCollins, 1996.

Grade levels: K–1.

While Katie and Rosie are eating some apples, Rosie swallows a few seeds. Big sister Katie tells Rosie that the seeds will grow in her stomach, sending branches out through her ears. Rosie imagines a variety of consequences, such as being unable to wear a hat or get on the bus. Finally, Rosie learns that she won't be growing an apple tree, and she actually misses the possibilities associated with having an apple tree grow out of her ears.

Activities

1. Ask the students if they have ever swallowed an apple, watermelon, or other type of seed. Share the warnings that any of the students received.

2. Read the book aloud. On the second reading, discuss what Rosie thought would happen after the tree grew in her stomach and through her ears. Make a two-column list on the board. In one column, list the effects of swallowing the seed. In the other column, list the effects of telling the lie. The chart might look something like the one on page 117.

Related books

Hall, Zoe. *The Apple Pie Tree.* Illustrated by Shari Halpern. New York: Scholastic, 1996.

Priceman, Marjorie. *How to Make an Apple Pie and See the World.* New York: Alfred A. Knopf, 1994.

Stevens, Jan Romero. *Carlos and the Squash Plant.* Illustrated by Jeanne Arnold. Flagstaff, Ariz.: Northland, 1993. (In both English and Spanish.)

From: Bridges to Reading, Grades K-3: Teaching Reading Skills with Children's Literature. © 1999 Suzanne I. Barchers. Teacher Ideas Press (800) 237-6124.

From: Bridges to Reading, Grades K-3: Teaching Reading Skills with Children's Literature. © 1999 Suzanne I. Barchers. Teacher Ideas Press (800) 237-6124.

Effect: Swallowing the Seed	Effect: Telling a Fib
Hats wouldn't fit.	Feeling sad.
Couldn't get on the school bus.	Having a hard time telling the truth.
Couldn't do somersaults and handstands.	Feeling sorry.
Couldn't jump rope.	Feeling glad when the truth is told.
Would have to go to the woodcutter.	

Text Structure: Cause and Effect

Priceman, Marjorie. *How to Make an Apple Pie and See the World.* New York: Alfred A. Knopf, 1994.

Grade levels: 2–3.

When a girl decides to make an apple pie, she goes to the market to buy the ingredients. But the market is closed, so she begins a journey to collect the ingredients. Among other places, she goes to Italy for the wheat, to France for eggs, and to Sri Lanka for cinnamon. Finally, she returns home and fixes the pie. Then she yearns for vanilla ice cream, but of course the market is *still* closed.

Activities

1. Ask the students if they know the ingredients needed to make an apple pie. List them on the board. Then ask the students where they would get them if they couldn't purchase them at a grocery store.

2. Read the book aloud. Using a globe or world map, locate all the countries that the girl visited.

3. Create a chart that lists the causes and the effects of the various steps to gathering the ingredients, as shown on page 119.

4. After completing the chart, discuss what will happen next in the book. List the steps involved in collecting the ingredients for ice cream and write a sequel to the book, *How to Make Vanilla Ice Cream and See the World.*

Related books

Hall, Zoe. *The Apple Pie Tree.* Illustrated by Shari Halpern. New York: Scholastic, 1996.

Lerner, Harriet, and Susan Goldhor. *What's So Terrible About Swallowing an Apple Seed?* Illustrated by Catharine O'Neil. New York: HarperCollins, 1996.

Stevens, Jan Romero. *Carlos and the Squash Plant.* Illustrated by Jeanne Arnold. Flagstaff, Ariz.: Northland, 1993. (In both English and Spanish.)

From: Bridges to Reading, Grades K–3: Teaching Reading Skills with Children's Literature. © 1999 Suzanne I. Barchers. Teacher Ideas Press (800) 237-6124.

From: Bridges to Reading, Grades K-3: Teaching Reading Skills with Children's Literature. © 1999 Suzanne I. Barchers. Teacher Ideas Press (800) 237-6124.

Text Structure: Cause and Effect

Cause	Effect
The market is closed.	The girl must collect the ingredients.
She needs wheat.	She goes to Italy on a ship.
She needs eggs.	She goes to France.
She needs cinnamon.	She goes to Sri Lanka.

Text Structure: Compare/Contrast

 Clement, Rod. *Just Another Ordinary Day.* New York: HarperCollins, 1995.

Grade levels: K–1.

Amanda gets up in the morning like other children, except that a servant awakens her. She dons wings to fly down to breakfast, where she eats a huge egg. A dinosaur drives her to school, where she learns from unusual teachers. Her day's activities continue—both ordinary and extraordinary in nature.

Activities

1. Discuss with the students how their typical day begins: how they awaken, what they eat, how they get to school.

2. Read the book aloud. Then create a chart that compares Amanda's day with their typical day. The chart might look something like the example on page 121.

3. Create another chart that shows how each student's typical day compares and contrasts with each other's. For example, most will eat breakfast, with some having cereal and others having pancakes. Some may come to school in a car while others come in a bus.

Related books

Egan, Tim. *Burnt Toast on Davenport Street.* Boston: Houghton Mifflin, 1997.

Feiffer, Jules. *Meanwhile . . . .* New York: HarperCollins, 1997.

Yorinks, Arthur. *Ugh.* Illustrated by Richard Egielski. New York: Farrar, Straus & Giroux, 1990.

120

From: Bridges to Reading, Grades K–3: Teaching Reading Skills with Children's Literature. © 1999 Suzanne I. Barchers. Teacher Ideas Press (800) 237-6124.

Amanda's Day	Similarities	Students' Day
Awakened by a servant.	Awakened by a person.	Awakened by a parent.
Dresses in wings.	Gets dressed.	Dresses in jeans.
Flies down to breakfast.	Goes to breakfast.	Walks to breakfast.
Eats a huge egg.	Eats an egg.	Eats a small egg.
Driven to school by a dinosaur.	Goes to school in a vehicle.	Goes to school in a car or bus.

From: Bridges to Reading, Grades K–3: Teaching Reading Skills with Children's Literature. © 1999 Suzanne I. Barchers. Teacher Ideas Press (800) 237-6124.

Appelbaum, Diana. *Cocoa Ice.* Illustrated by Holly Meade. New York: Orchard, 1997.

Grade levels: 2–3.

A young girl describes life on her island, where the family harvests cocoa beans. After the beans dry, they roast and crush them with a mortar. Finally, her father trades some beans for ice from a ship, and they have a treat of cocoa ice. In the second half of the book a young girl in Maine describes how ice forms in the river and is harvested for shipment to the Caribbean, where her father trades it for cocoa beans.

Activities

1. Show the students the map in the inside cover of the book. Discuss the two locations—Maine and Santo Domingo—asking the students how they would be different.

2. Read the story aloud, allowing time to enjoy the illustrations.

3. Brainstorm all the features of the two areas of the world that can be compared. For example, climate, dress, and diet. Create a chart that contrasts these two areas with your environment. List the features in a chart such as in the example on page 123.

4. Discuss the features that each place has in common.

Related books

Garay, Luis. *Pedrito's Day.* New York: Orchard, 1997.

Gershator, Phillis. *Sweet, Sweet Fig Banana.* Illustrated by Fritz Millevoix. Morton Grove, Ill.: Whitman, 1996.

Tchana, Katrin Hyman, and Louis Tchana Pami. *Oh, No, Toto!* Illustrated by Colin Bootman. New York: Scholastic, 1997.

Torres, Leyla. *Saturday Sancocho.* New York: Farrar, Straus & Giroux, 1995.

From: Bridges to Reading, Grades K–3: Teaching Reading Skills with Children's Literature. © 1999 Suzanne I. Barchers. Teacher Ideas Press (800) 237-6124.

Features	Santo Domingo	Maine	Your Home
Climate	Warm all year	Cold winters	
Dress	Colorful, light dress	Heavy, warm clothes	
Diet	Fish, coconuts	Apple pies	

From: Bridges to Reading, Grades K-3: Teaching Reading Skills with Children's Literature. © 1999 Suzanne I. Barchers. Teacher Ideas Press (800) 237-6124.

Berger, Melvin. *Chirping Crickets.* Illustrated by Megan Lloyd. New York: HarperCollins, 1998.

Grade levels: K–1.

Did you know that the crickets you hear chirping are all males? They are calling the females to them. Learn how crickets make the chirping noise, where their ears are (under their knees of their front legs), how they mate, how nymphs grow, how they see, and how they feel. This informative book will fascinate young students.

Activities

1. Ask the students if they have ever heard a cricket chirping. Can they describe or replicate the sound?

2. Read aloud Eric Carle's *The Very Quiet Cricket* (see the "Related books" section below). Does the cricket noise at the end of the book sound like crickets they have heard at night?

3. Before reading Berger's book aloud, bring in several nail files in preparation for the activity in the book. Ask the students to describe a cricket, listing all the descriptive words they use on the board. Then begin reading the book aloud.

4. Have the students try the activity in the book with the nail file and paper.

5. After reading through page 11, have the students describe how the cricket hears.

6. After reading through page 17, have the students describe how the nymph molts.

7. After reading through page 23, have the students describe everything they have learned about the appearance of crickets.

8. Try some of the activities at the end of the book.

Related books

Carle, Eric. *The Very Quiet Cricket.* New York: Putnam, 1990.

Esbensen, Barbara Juster. *Sponges Are Skeletons.* Illustrated by Holly Keller. New York: HarperCollins, 1993.

Heiligman, Deborah. *From Caterpillar to Butterfly.* Illustrated by Bari Weissman. New York: HarperCollins, 1996.

Jenkins, Priscilla Belz. *A Safe Home for Manatees.* Illustrated by Martin Classen. New York: HarperCollins, 1997.

Pfeffer, Wendy. *What's It Like to Be a Fish?* New York: HarperCollins, 1996.

From: Bridges to Reading, Grades K–3: Teaching Reading Skills with Children's Literature. © 1999 Suzanne I. Barchers. Teacher Ideas Press (800) 237-6124.

From: Bridges to Reading, Grades K-3: Teaching Reading Skills with Children's Literature. © 1999 Suzanne I. Barchers. Teacher Ideas Press (800) 237-6124.

Winkleman, Katherine K. *Police Patrol.* Illustrated by John S. Winkleman. New York: Walker, 1996.

Grade levels: 2–3.

In this informative book, readers learn about a variety of aspects of police work. Beginning with the police station, the book discusses the patrol officers, the arrest process, correctional institutions, detectives, the crime lab, fingerprints, canine partners, the bomb squad, undercover police, and various special units. The book concludes with safety tips and emergency directions.

Activities

1. Before reading the book, brainstorm everything the students know about the police force. Ask the students to describe a variety of items: a police uniform, a police car, a jail. Make arrangements for a visit to a police station or to have a police officer visit the classroom.

2. Read aloud the first main section of the book, which focuses on the police station. These two pages contain several descriptive paragraphs. First, read each paragraph aloud without showing the illustrations. Then ask the students to describe how they think each area will look based on the description given. Note that, in some cases, such as understanding how a gunport operates, the illustration is necessary for understanding. How could this paragraph have been made more descriptive, making the illustration unnecessary?

3. Read the next two pages, which focus on patrol officers. Discuss the paragraph that describes the practice of putting a photo in the police hats. Then show the illustration. Could the paragraph have been made more descriptive so that the illustration would be unnecessary? Examine the illustration of the police uniform. Discuss how effective labeling can eliminate the need for extra words in the description.

4. Continue through the book, choosing paragraphs to expand on for description. When finished, take a field trip to a police station or interview an officer and compare the book's descriptions with what they see or learn.

Related books

Gibbons, Gail. *Emergency!* New York: Holiday House, 1994.

Mayer, Mercer. *Policeman Critter.* New York: Simon & Schuster, 1986.

Axelrod, Amy. *Pigs in the Pantry.* Illustrated by Sharon McGinley-Nally. New York: Simon & Schuster, 1997.

Grade levels: K–1.

Mrs. Pig doesn't feel well, so Mr. Pig and the piglets decide to make her favorite dish. They realize that they don't know much about cooking but believe it can't be very hard. They find a recipe for Firehouse Chili and begin to make the recipe. Predictably, they create chaos by not following the recipe. But the arrival of the fire department saves the day, and everyone shares the Firehouse Chili.

Activities

1. Read the story aloud with the students. Then make a list of all the steps Mr. Pig followed.

2. Next, discuss the question posed by the author at the end of the story, asking what Mr. Pig needs to learn about cooking. Talk about the mistakes he made, returning to the recipe to discuss the steps he should have taken.

3. Make a numbered list of the steps Mr. Pig should have taken.

4. Speculate on what happens next in the story. Who do the students think will clean up the mess? Have them make a list of all the steps that need to be taken to clean up the kitchen.

5. Tell the students that they are going to make a list of rules for the kitchen. Tell them to start with the most important first. Post the numbered list.

6. Plan to make Firehouse Chili in the classroom. Make a list of everything that needs to happen to have a successful cooking experience. Make the chili and enjoy eating it.

Related books

Christelow, Eileen. *Don't Wake Up Mama!* New York: Trumpet, 1992.

Day, Alexandra. *Frank and Ernest.* New York: Scholastic, 1988.

Hutchins, Pat. *The Doorbell Rang.* New York: Greenwillow, 1986.

Robinson, Fay. *Pizza Soup.* Illustrated by Ann Iosa. Chicago: Childrens Press, 1993.

From: Bridges to Reading, Grades K-3: Teaching Reading Skills with Children's Literature. © 1999 Suzanne I. Barchers. Teacher Ideas Press (800) 237-6124.

From: Bridges to Reading, Grades K–3: Teaching Reading Skills with Children's Literature. © 1999 Suzanne I. Barchers. Teacher Ideas Press (800) 237-6124.

Cole, Joanna, and Stephanie Calmenson. With Michael Street. *Marbles: 101 Ways to Play.* Illustrated by Alan Tiegreen. New York: Morrow Junior Books, 1998.

Grade levels: 2–3.

This complete book on playing marbles begins with a history of marbles. It describes the basics, including marble stakes and surfaces. After reading a section on how to play marbles, readers can learn about circle games, hole games, shooting games, and various other games. Illustrations provide further clarity to this informative book.

Activities

1. Read aloud the history of marbles and the section entitled "Before You Begin." Discuss the tips for shooting. Discuss the terms listed on page 27.

2. Have the students form small groups. Then have each group write out the directions for how to play marbles. Tell them to be sure the steps are clearly worded.

3. Have marbles available. Using one group's directions, let the students play a game of marbles.

4. Tell the students that they are going to learn the official version, Ringer, as it is described in the book. Photocopy pages 30 and 31 onto overhead transparencies. Take the students through the steps, from 1 to 7. Compare the book's steps with those of the students. Were the versions the same? Discuss what happens when directions aren't clear.

5. Play marbles again, using the official version. Then have the students choose other versions to play. Have them follow the directions sequentially.

6. Have the students choose a playground game and write the directions down in steps. Can they make the directions clear and orderly?

Related books

Greenaway, Kate. *Kate Greenaway's Book of Games.* London: Grange Books, 1993.

Lankford, Mary D. *Dominoes Around the World.* Illustrated by Karen Dugan. New York: Morrow, 1998.

Petričić, Dušan. *Let's Play: Traditional Games of Childhood.* Illustrated by Camilla Gryski. Toronto: Kids Can Press, 1995.

127

Murphy, Stuart J. *A Fair Bear Share.* Illustrated by John Speirs. New York: HarperCollins, 1998.

Grade levels: K–1.

Mama Bear sends the little bears out to collect nuts, berries, and seeds. She promises to bake her special pie, giving all the bears a "fair bear share." But one bear chooses to play instead of helping. When Mama Bear tells them that there aren't quite enough nuts, berries, and seeds for the pie, the little sister quickly gathers her share. Then they all enjoy the special pie.

Activities

1. This book combines math with the story line. Each time the bears return with their baskets of nuts, seeds, and berries, their mother adds up the items, regrouping them to add them. Be prepared to discuss the math as appropriate for your group.

2. Begin reading the book aloud. After reading pages 4 and 5, discuss the problem that they have: gathering enough nuts, berries, and seeds for the pie.

3. After reading pages 9 and 10, discuss the total number of nuts gathered. Note that the fourth cub had zero nuts. Will this be a problem? What might the solution be?

4. After reading through page 19, discuss how the fourth cub still hadn't contributed to the pie. What is a possible solution? Can the students predict what might happen next?

5. After finishing the book, discuss the main problem: finding the ingredients for the pie. Discuss the other main problem: that the fourth bear wanted to play. Ask the students if they can think of other solutions for the story. Discuss those possibilities.

Related books

Hutchins, Pat. *The Doorbell Rang.* New York: Greenwillow, 1986.

Murphy, Stuart J. *Give Me Half!* Illustrated by G. Brian Karas. New York: HarperCollins, 1996.

Pinczes, Elinor. *One Hundred Hungry Ants.* Illustrated by Bonnie MacKain. New York: Scholastic, 1993.

Ziefert, Harriet. *A Dozen Dozens.* Illustrated by Chris Demarest. New York: Putnam, 1998.

From: Bridges to Reading, Grades K–3: Teaching Reading Skills with Children's Literature. © 1999 Suzanne I. Barchers. Teacher Ideas Press (800) 237-6124.

Lerner, Carol. *My Backyard Garden.* New York: Morrow, 1998.

Grade levels: 2–3.

This colorful resource discusses how to get started with gardening: choosing a site, deciding on the size, planning the garden, keeping records, choosing tools, preparing the ground, and dealing with pets and wildlife. Then it provides a month-by-month guide to managing the garden from March to October. An index increases the usefulness of the book.

Activities

1. Each of the introductory sections provides a problem that the gardener must consider: finding the right place, managing the watering, choosing the size of the garden, and so forth. Use these sections to discuss how the author provides solutions to the various problems.

2. Create charts to list the problems and solutions. Use the chart below as a model.

3. Plan a small classroom garden. If the students go on vacation during the summer, plan with them how to solve the problem of who will take care of the garden. (Possible solutions include: plant the garden in pots students can take home; assign students to take turns tending the garden during the summer; plant spring crops only.)

Problem	Solution(s)
Vegetable plants need sunshine.	Choose a spot with 6 hours of exposure to direct sun. Stay away from buildings and trees.
Plants need water.	Choose a spot with good drainage. Make raised beds so water drains away. Make sure water is nearby.
Big gardens require a lot of work.	Start small. A good size is 20 square feet.

From: Bridges to Reading, Grades K-3: Teaching Reading Skills with Children's Literature. © 1999 Suzanne I. Barchers. Teacher Ideas Press (800) 237-6124.

Text Structure: Problem/Solution

Related books

Carlson, Laurie. *Green Thumbs: A Kid's Activity Guide to Indoor and Outdoor Gardening.* Chicago: Chicago Review Press, 1995.

Markham, Ursula. *The Children's Gardening Book.* London: Breese Books, 1993.

Scott, Emily, and Catherine Duffy. *Dinner from Dirt: Ten Meals Kids Can Grow and Cook.* Salt Lake City, Utah: Gibbs-Smith, 1998.

From: Bridges to Reading, Grades K-3: Teaching Reading Skills with Children's Literature. © 1999 Suzanne I. Barchers. Teacher Ideas Press (800) 237-6124.

From: Bridges to Reading, Grades K–3: Teaching Reading Skills with Children's Literature. © 1999 Suzanne I. Barchers. Teacher Ideas Press (800) 237-6124.

Bunting, Eve. *Flower Garden.* Illustrated by Kathryn Hewitt. New York: Trumpet, 1994.

Grade levels: K–1.

A young girl and her father go shopping for groceries and flowers. When they get home, they fill a box with planting mix. Then they plant the flowers in the box, placing it on the windowsill above the street. Passersby, along with butterflies, enjoy the box. Finally, the girl's mother comes home to enjoy birthday cake and her birthday present—a garden window box.

Activities

1. Ask the students to list all the steps involved in planting a flower in a pot. Write their directions on the board.

2. Read the story aloud, taking time to enjoy the colorful illustrations.

3. Then ask the students to recall all the steps the little girl and her father took to create the flower box. Write the steps on the board. Then reread the story. Did the students recall all the steps correctly and in the correct order? Fill in any missing steps.

4. Compare the list of steps from the story with the list the students created before listening to the story.

5. Work with the whole class to write a paragraph that lists the steps to create a flower box. Use the following as a template, adding sentences as appropriate:

    To make a flower box, first you _____.

    Next you _____.

    After gathering the soil and box, you _____.

    Finally, you _____.

Related books

Cushman, Doug. *Mouse and Mole and the Year-Round Garden.* New York: Trumpet, 1994.

Ehlert, Lois. *Growing Vegetable Soup.* San Diego, Calif.: Harcourt Brace & Company, 1987.

Ernst, Lisa Campbell. *Miss Penny and Mr. Grubbs.* New York: Simon & Schuster, 1991, 1995.

Hennessy, B. G. *Jake Baked the Cake.* Illustrated by Mary Morgan. New York: Viking Penguin, 1990, 1992.

Grade levels: 2–3.

Everyone prepares for a grand wedding. The wedding dress is sewn, the champagne arrives, the gifts are stacked. During all the preparations, Jake bakes the cake. Finally the wedding begins, and Jake is still baking the cake. But the spectacular cake is ready, just in time.

Activities

1. Ask the students if they have ever attended or participated in a wedding. List everything on the board that the students can remember about the wedding. Ask them to list all the things that must be done before a wedding. Write these on the board.

2. Read this short book aloud. When finished, tell the students that you are going to read the story again. Divide the class in half. Tell one half that they will be responsible for remembering all the events related to the wedding. Tell the other half that they should pay particular attention to everything that Jake is doing.

3. After rereading the story, ask the first half of the class to list all the events that led up to the wedding in the order that they appeared in the story. Write the list on the board.

4. Then have the second half of the class list all the steps Jake took in preparing the cake.

5. Read the story again. Confirm the lists as you read. Rearrange any steps as necessary, discussing the order presented in the book. Discuss how the author integrated the steps of the two stories.

Related books

Hines, Anna Grossnickle. *Daddy Makes the Best Spaghetti.* New York: Trumpet, 1986.

Robart, Rose. *The Cake That Mack Ate.* Illustrated by Maryann Kovalski. Boston: Little, Brown, 1986.

Robinson, Fay. *Pizza Soup.* Illustrated by Ann Iosa. Chicago: Childrens Press, 1993.

From: Bridges to Reading, Grades K–3: Teaching Reading Skills with Children's Literature. © 1999 Suzanne I. Barchers. Teacher Ideas Press (800) 237-6124.

From: Bridges to Reading, Grades K–3: Teaching Reading Skills with Children's Literature. © 1999 Suzanne I. Barchers. Teacher Ideas Press (800) 237-6124.

Cole, Henry. *I Took a Walk.* New York: Greenwillow, 1998.

Grade levels: K–1.

A youngster goes for a walk on a spring morning. While following a path, the narrator lists all the observed insects, animals, plants, and tracks. The foldout pages encourage the reader to look for each item on the list. The habitats include the woods, a meadow, a stream, and a pond. A guide at the end of the book provides an identification key.

Activities

1. Read the book aloud, folding out the pages. Search for the members of each habitat, pointing each out on the illustrations. Discuss how they live, their environment, and the plants they need to survive.

2. Using small sticky notes, write each word from the lists at the end of the book on a separate note. Label the pages with the notes. Check accuracy by using the identification key on the last page.

3. Choose another environment, such as the mountains or deserts. Then choose a habitat within that environment, such as a den, a burrow, or a nest. Create a mural or diorama that includes plants and animals from that habitat. Label the animals and plants on the mural or diorama.

Related books

Duncan, Beverly K. *Explore the Wild: A Nature Search-and-Find Book.* New York: HarperCollins, 1996.

Fleming, Denise. *In the Small, Small Pond.* New York: Henry Holt, 1993.

Krupinski, Loretta. *Into the Woods: A Woodland Scrapbook.* New York: HarperCollins, 1997.

Wallace, Marianne D. *America's Deserts.* Golden, Colo.: Fulcrum, 1996.

———. *America's Mountains.* Golden, Colo.: Fulcrum, 1999.

Hoban, Tana. *So Many Circles, So Many Squares.* New York: Greenwillow, 1998.

Grade levels: 2–3.

Browsing through this wordless book is like taking a photographic walk with Tana Hoban. On the way, one can see circles and squares in everything from bicycles to smokestacks to a waffle. The color photographs direct the eye to view previously unnoticed shapes everywhere in the environment.

Activities

1. Share the book while discussing all the circles and squares found in the pictures.

2. On the second reading, make a chart that identifies all the circles and squares, as in the example below.

3. On the third reading, look for other shapes. This provides a good opportunity to look for trapezoids, parallelograms, ovals, and triangles. Add them to the chart.

4. Take a walk around the school, playground, or neighborhood. Make a list of all the shapes that can be seen. If possible, take photographs and make a similar book of shapes.

Circles	Squares
p. 1: bicycle tires	p. 2: street pavers, center of hubcap
p. 2: car tire, lug nuts	p. 3: box holding reflector
p. 3: reflectors	p. 4: frame, hole
p. 5: radishes	p. 6: wire squares on basket
p. 6: onion	p. 7: screens

From: Bridges to Reading, Grades K-3: Teaching Reading Skills with Children's Literature. © 1999 Suzanne I. Barchers. Teacher Ideas Press (800) 237-6124.

Related books

Dodds, Dayle Ann. *The Shape of Things.* Illustrated by Julie Lacome. Cambridge, Mass.: Candlewick Press, 1994.

Henkes, Kevin. *Circle Dogs.* Illustrated by Dan Yaccarino. New York: Greenwillow, 1998.

Hoban, Tana. *Look Book.* New York: Greenwillow, 1997.

———. *Take Another Look.* New York: Greenwillow, 1981.

Murphy, Stuart J. *Circus Shapes.* Illustrated by Edward Miller. New York: HarperCollins, 1998.

Wilson, April. *Look Again!* New York: Dial, 1992.

From: Bridges to Reading, Grades K–3: Teaching Reading Skills with Children's Literature. © 1999 Suzanne I. Barchers. Teacher Ideas Press (800) 237-6124.

Conrad, Pam. *Animal Lingo.* Illustrated by Barbara Bustetter Falk. New York: HarperCollins, 1995.

Grade levels: K–1.

Did you know that a cow in Holland says *Boo,* not *Moo?,* and in Turkey, the dogs say *Hav! Hav!* Children will delight in and appreciate this collection of animal sounds from around the world. The illustrations provide a sense of the country in addition to showing the featured animal.

Activities

1. Before sharing this book, ask the students to tell you what a dog sounds like. Try to get as many responses as possible: *ruff, bark, yip, grr, whine,* and so forth. Talk about how dogs make different sounds depending on what they are trying to communicate.

2. Read the book, letting the students help you decide the appropriate pronunciations. Before showing the last page, have the students predict what the children say at nighttime.

3. Using a world map, find the countries that are represented in *Animal Lingo.* Have the students draw each animal on a sticky note, add its sound, and place it on the map on the appropriate country.

4. Sing "Old MacDonald Had a Farm" with the traditional sounds (see Tracey Campbell Pearson's entry in the "Related books" section below). Then list the animals and sounds from *Animal Lingo* on the board and sing the song again, using the animals and sounds from around the world.

Related books

Carle, Eric. *The Very Busy Spider.* New York: Putnam, 1987.

Hutchins, Pat. *Little Pink Pig.* New York: Greenwillow, 1994.

Lewison, Wendy Cheyette. *Going to Sleep on the Farm.* Illustrated by Juan Wijngaard. New York: Trumpet, 1992.

Pearson, Tracey Campbell. *Old MacDonald Had a Farm.* New York: Dial, 1984.

Ziefert, Harriet, and Simms Taback. *Who Said Moo?* New York: HarperCollins, 1996.

From: Bridges to Reading, Grades K-3: Teaching Reading Skills with Children's Literature. © 1999 Suzanne I. Barchers. Teacher Ideas Press (800) 237-6124.

From: Bridges to Reading, Grades K–3: Teaching Reading Skills with Children's Literature. © 1999 Suzanne I. Barchers. Teacher Ideas Press (800) 237-6124.

Vocabulary: Appreciating Words

Dorros, Arthur. *Abuela.* New York: Dutton, 1991.

Grade levels: 2–3.

A little girl and her grandmother pretend to fly over the rooftops of the city talking about all the wonderful things and people they would see. The colorful illustrations provide a fascinating perspective on their city life.

Activities

1. Read aloud the book and discuss the use of the Spanish words. Decide on the English words for the Spanish. Write them on sticky notes, place them over the Spanish words, and read the text again. Discuss the beauty that the Spanish words add to the reading of the book.

2. Discuss all the sights in your city or community. List everything you would see from above. List descriptive words that would tell about the sights and people. Use these words to create newsletter articles or stories about your community.

3. Have the students create a map as they envision how their community would look from above. Label the buildings, parks, homes, and streets. Use both English and Spanish for the labels if possible. Display the maps in the classroom.

4. Choose another language that is represented in the classroom or that is of interest to the students. Create a similar map using the other language. Discuss how words from other languages are drawn into common use, such as *adios*. Keep a list of words the students identify that come from other languages.

Related books

Fanelli, Sara. *My Map Book.* New York: HarperCollins, 1995.

Garay, Luis. *Pedrito's Day.* New York: Orchard, 1997.

Gershator, Phillis. *Sweet, Sweet Fig Banana.* Illustrated by Fritz Millevoix. Morton Grove, Ill.: Whitman, 1996.

Heide, Florence Parry, and Roxanne Heide Pierce. *Tío Armando.* Illustrated by Ann Grifalconi. New York: Lothrop, Lee and Shepard, 1998.

Vocabulary: Direct Instruction

Most, Bernard. *There's an Ant in Anthony.* New York: Morrow, 1980.

Grade levels: K–1.

One day Anthony was learning how to spell his name in school. He discovers the *ant* in Anthony and sets out on a journey to discover if *ant* appears in other places. He doesn't always find an *ant*, but he has many successes. He even finds *ants* in his *pants!* Finally, he has found enough and he goes home that inst*ant*.

Activities

1. Students will enjoy this clever book as they look for the word *ant* in the various words on the pages. Read the book through, enjoying Anthony's antics. During the second reading, list all the *ant* words on the board. How many did Anthony find? Can the students think of other words that include *ant*?

2. Choose another simple word, such as *rat* or *hat*, and start collecting words that include it. Create illustrations that use the same technique of using black and white except for the key word.

3. Examine each student's first, middle, and last name. Can the students find words in their names? During the next few weeks, have them keep a list of words they find that contain their word.

4. Encourage students to find little words in other words during their reading. Keep lists of words they have found.

Related books

Krudwig, Vickie Leigh. *Cucumber Soup.* Illustrated by Craig McFarland Brown. Golden, Colo.: Fulcrum Kids, 1998.

Pinczes, Elinor J. *One Hundred Hungry Ants.* Illustrated by Bonnie MacKain. New York: Scholastic, 1983.

———. *A Remainder of One.* Illustrated by Bonnie MacKain. New York: Scholastic, 1995.

Rattigan, Jama Kim. *Truman's Aunt Farm.* Illustrated by G. Brian Karas. Boston: Houghton Mifflin, 1984.

From: Bridges to Reading, Grades K-3: Teaching Reading Skills with Children's Literature. © 1999 Suzanne I. Barchers. Teacher Ideas Press (800) 237-6124.

West, Colin. *One Day in the Jungle.* Cambridge, Mass.: Candlewick Press, 1995.
Grade levels: 2–3.

A butterfly has a little sneeze. The next day, the lizard has a not-quite-so-little sneeze. With each subsequently larger sneeze, an appropriate adjective is used, until the elephant has a gigantic sneeze.

Activities

1. Read aloud the book and discuss the use of the words that compare the sizes of the sneezes, making a list on the board. Create clusters or lists of words that compare feelings (okay, good, great, wonderful, fabulous, fair, so-so).

2. Create a group story using a cluster of comparison words.

3. Use the words to create a semantic gradient. Have the students decide the order of the words as they relate to each other. Opinions may vary as to the degree of meanings. For an example of a semantic gradient, arrange the following words from the smallest to the biggest:

enormous	smallest	tiny _____
microscopic		_____
middle-sized		_____
huge		_____
little		_____
large		_____
tiny	biggest	_____

Related books

Edwards, Richard. *Something's Coming!* Illustrated by Dana Kubick. Cambridge, Mass.: Candlewick Press, 1995.

McMillan, Bruce. *Super Super Superwords.* New York: Lothrop, Lee and Shepard, 1989.

Murphy, Stuart J. *The Best Bug Parade.* Illustrated by Holly Keller. New York: Harper-Collins, 1996.

Thaler, Mike. *In the Middle of the Puddle.* Illustrated by Bruce Degen. New York: Harper & Row, 1988.

Waddell, Martin. *Once There Were Giants.* Illustrated by Penny Dale. Cambridge, Mass.: Candlewick Press, 1989.

From: Bridges to Reading, Grades K–3: Teaching Reading Skills with Children's Literature. © 1999 Suzanne I. Barchers. Teacher Ideas Press (800) 237-6124.

Branley, Franklyn M. *Day Light, Night Light: Where Light Comes From.* Illustrated by Stacey Schuett. New York: HarperCollins, 1975, 1998.

Grade levels: 2–3.

Light comes in the morning and disappears at night, although it is hard to find total darkness. The role of the sun and the stars are discussed, as well as that of reflected light on the moon. The process of light traveling and the role of heat in creating light are explored in simple terms. The book concludes with speculation on where the reader could find total darkness.

Activities

1. Before sharing the book, make a list of the content-related words in the book. Consider including the following words on the list: *light, sun, moon, stars, heat, bulb, candle, electricity, bounce, reflection, travel, candle, darkness.*

2. Write the content-related words on the board or on chart paper. Tell the students that before reading the book you are going to play a game called "Connect Two" with some of the words in the book. Show the students the list of words. Tell them to choose two words that go together, then explain why they would connect their choices. Student views may vary concerning which words should be connected. Use colored chalk to show the various choices.

3. Read the book aloud, discussing the vocabulary words as necessary. Return to the list of connected words. Would the students change the connections? Use another color of chalk to show new connections.

4. Ask the students to add words to your list. Then play "Connect Three" with the words, repeating the process of justifying why the three words should be connected.

5. This process can be used with any informational text. When working in a textbook, assign sections to students and have them create their own word list for others to connect.

Related books

Lauber, Patricia. *What Do You See and How Do You See It? Exploring Light, Color and Vision.* Photographs by Leonard Lessin. New York: Crown, 1994.

Tomecek, Steve. *Bouncing and Bending Light.* Illustrated by Arnie Ten. New York: W. H. Freeman, 1995.

From: Bridges to Reading, Grades K–3: Teaching Reading Skills with Children's Literature. © 1999 Suzanne I. Barchers. Teacher Ideas Press (800) 237-6124.

From: Bridges to Reading, Grades K–3: Teaching Reading Skills with Children's Literature. © 1999 Suzanne I. Barchers. Teacher Ideas Press (800) 237-6124.

 Fowler, Susi Greg. *Beautiful.* Illustrated by Jim Fowler. New York: Greenwillow, 1998.

Grade levels: 2–3.

Uncle George, a wonderful gardener, gives his nephew a birthday gift of gardening tools and seeds. After helping his nephew plant his garden, Uncle George leaves for treatment of his illness. While the garden grows, Uncle George encourages his nephew from a distance. Finally, when Uncle George returns home to die, his nephew brings the beautiful flowers to him to enjoy.

Activities

1. Many flower names originated from Greek or Latin. For example, the Latin word *columba* means "dove" and can be found in the flower name columbine. Use the library to find listings of the origins of plant names.

2. Create riddles using the original plant names. For example:

   I shine as *anth* (flower) because of my *khrusos* (gold). What am I?

   —Chrysanthemum.

3. Research the common names of plants and discuss why they were given those names. Some good names to research include: lipstick plants, blazing star, basket of gold, silverdollar gum, beard tongue, bottle tree, mirror plant, balloon flower, hoop pine, baseball plant, cup and saucer, bleeding heart, dogtooth violet, flytrap, catchfly, snapdragon, helmet flower, baby's tears, pocketbook plant, mouse-ear, cat tail, crowfoot, angel's hair, Jack in the pulpit, Queen Anne's lace, damask rose, spindle tree, ice plant, and zebra plant.

Related books

Gerstein, Mordicai. *Daisy's Garden.* Illustrated by Susan Yard Harris. New York: Hyperion, 1995.

Lerner, Carol. *My Backyard Garden.* New York: Morrow, 1998.

Mallet, David. *Inch by Inch: The Garden Song.* Illustrated by Ora Eitan. New York: HarperCollins, 1995.

Thomas, Elizabeth. *Green Beans.* Illustrated by Vicki Jo Redenbaugh. Minneapolis, Minn.: Carolrhoda, 1992.

Willard, Nancy. *Cracked Corn and Snow Ice Cream.* Illustrated by Jane Dyer. San Diego, Calif.: Harcourt Brace, 1997.

Heiligman, Deborah. *From Caterpillar to Butterfly.* Illustrated by Bari Weissman. New York: HarperCollins, 1996.

Grade levels: K–1.

When a caterpillar comes to school in a jar, the class learns how a caterpillar grows and splits its skin. They watch it make the chrysalis, waiting until the butterfly emerges. Finally, they release the butterfly to enjoy life outdoors. The book concludes with examples of different kinds of butterflies to look for and butterfly centers to visit.

Activities

1. Before reading the book aloud, write a variety of words from the book on the board, such as *caterpillar*, *butterfly*, *larva*, *molt*, *silk*, *chrysalis*, *pupa*, *nectar*, and *proboscis*.

2. Include in the list a variety of words that do not directly relate to the book, for example, *spider*, *web*, *invertebrate*, *pond*, *vibrate*, *spin*, *den*.

3. Explain to the students that they are going to play a game, "Exclusion Brainstorming," before hearing the story. Tell them that you have written a lot of words on the board but that some don't fit with the story about the butterfly. Ask them to guess which words don't fit. Circle those words.

4. After reading the story aloud, return to the list. Were some words excluded that should have been retained? If so, erase the circles. If some were not excluded, circle those words. Then erase all the words that didn't fit the story. Return to the book to confirm the choices if necessary. This process can be used to reinforce vocabulary for any informational book.

Related books

Berger, Melvin. *Chirping Crickets.* Illustrated by Megan Lloyd. New York: HarperCollins, 1998.

Markle, Sandra. *Creepy, Crawly Baby Bugs.* New York: Walker, 1996.

Otto, Carolyn. *What Color Is Camouflage?* Illustrated by Megan Lloyd. New York: HarperCollins, 1996.

From: Bridges to Reading, Grades K-3: Teaching Reading Skills with Children's Literature. © 1999 Suzanne I. Barchers. Teacher Ideas Press (800) 237-6124.

From: Bridges to Reading, Grades K-3: Teaching Reading Skills with Children's Literature. © 1999 Suzanne I. Barchers. Teacher Ideas Press (800) 237-6124.

Lauber, Patricia. *You're Aboard Spaceship Earth.* Illustrated by Holly Keller. New York: HarperCollins, 1996.

Grade levels: 2–3.

When a space shuttle takes off, everything the crew needs is on board just as those of us on Earth have everything we need as we travel through space. The use of water and oxygen is described. Nature's cycle of decomposition and its contribution to our food is also described in simple terms.

Activities

1. Have the students make a list of everything they would need if they were to travel into outer space on a space shuttle.

2. Next, have the students make a list of everything they need to survive on Earth. Compare the two lists.

3. Read aloud the book. Have the students add to both lists. Do they need the same things for survival on Earth and in outer space?

4. Discuss with the students if they think we will always have what we need to live on spaceship earth. Ask them what they think should happen to make sure that they always have what they need. Make a list of things the class can do to ensure the survival of spaceship earth.

5. Have the students read about other planets. Can any of them sustain life? Which planet comes closest to sustaining life? What would the students need to supply to survive? Write a description of the ideal planet.

Related books

Branley, Franklyn M. *Floating in Space.* Illustrated by True Kelley. New York: Harper-Collins, 1998.

———. *The Planets in Our Solar System.* Illustrated by Kevin O'Malley. New York: HarperCollins, 1998.

Simon, Seymour. *Comets, Meteors, and Asteroids.* New York: Morrow, 1994.

Wordplay: Alliteration

Gustafson, Scott. *Alphabet Soup: A Feast of Letters.* Shelton, Conn.: Greenwich Workshop, 1990, 1994.

Grade levels: K–1.

Otter's new house is empty except for a soup pot. He decides to have a housewarming party, asking his guests to bring something for his soup pot. His 26 closest friends come, from Armadillo, who brings asparagus, to Zebra, who brings zucchini. After the soup cooks, they all enjoy eating it, making Otter's new house a home.

Activities

1. Read aloud the story. During the second reading, discuss the use of alliteration for each of the animals.

2. Make a chart that lists the animals and the food each brought. Discuss other foods that each animal could have brought. For example, Armadillo could have brought artichokes and bear could have brought beef.

3. Use the dictionary to look up any items, such as kumquats and krill, that might be unfamiliar to the students.

4. Create an alphabet meal using only the first names of the students in your classroom. For example, if you have an Alex in your classroom, he might bring in apples. Let the students decide what they are going to bring for a true potluck—just like Otter's!

Animal	Food	Other Foods
Armadillo	Asparagus	Artichokes
Bear	Bread	Beef
Cricket	Crackers	

From: Bridges to Reading, Grades K–3: Teaching Reading Skills with Children's Literature. © 1999 Suzanne I. Barchers. Teacher Ideas Press (800) 237-6124.

Related books

Bayer, Jane. *A My Name Is Alice.* Illustrated by Steven Kellogg. New York: Trumpet, 1984.

Edwards, Pamela Duncan. *Four Famished Foxes and Fosdyke.* Illustrated by Henry Cole. New York: HarperCollins, 1995.

———. *Some Smug Slug.* Illustrated by Henry Cole. New York: HarperCollins, 1996.

Walker, John. *Ridiculous Rhymes from A to Z.* Illustrated by David Catrow. New York: Henry Holt, 1995.

Yates, Gene. *The Elephant Alphabet Book.* Chicago: Kidsbooks, 1995.

From: Bridges to Reading, Grades K-3: Teaching Reading Skills with Children's Literature. © 1999 Suzanne I. Barchers. Teacher Ideas Press (800) 237-6124.

Wordplay: Alliteration

Edwards, Pamela Duncan. *Four Famished Foxes and Fosdyke.* Illustrated by Henry Cole. New York: HarperCollins, 1995.

Grade levels: 2–3.

When the foxes' mom leaves for five days in Florida, the four fox kits decide they want to filch fowl from the nearby farmyard. Fosdyke prefers fixing food to filching. The fox kits fail repeatedly, while Fosdyke fixes a variety of foods, such as flan, French fries, and fish. Finally, the fox kits give up and they all enjoy fondue. This is a delightful read-aloud, deriving its humor from alliteration and a great plot.

Activities

1. Read the book aloud. Allow the students to fill in words as they listen. During the second reading, list a variety of examples of alliteration on the board. Find the 60 objects in the book that begin with the letter *f*. Then list all the foods mentioned in the story.

2. Create a class story using a similar plot but with another letter of the alphabet. For example, 11 elephants may decide they want to escape to Estonia while their father cooks foods that start with the letter *e* (eels, escargot, elk, eggs, egret, and so forth).

3. Celebrate the book by cooking French toast, following routine safety procedures.

French Toast

6 eggs	1 tablespoon confectioners' sugar
1/4 cup milk	8 to 10 slices bread
1/2 teaspoon vanilla	1/4 cup melted butter
1/2 teaspoon cinnamon	Confectioners' sugar, syrup (optional)

1. Mix the eggs, milk, vanilla, cinnamon, and 1 tablespoon confectioners' sugar.
2. Heat a griddle to medium-high or 375 degrees.
3. Place 1/2 teaspoon melted butter on the griddle.
4. Dip a slice of bread into the egg mixture. Coat both sides well. Hold the bread slice over the bowl until it stops dripping. Place the bread on the butter. Repeat with remaining bread.
5. Grill each slice for approximately 1 minute or until brown. Turn and grill other side. Remove and place on serving plates. Serve with confectioners' sugar or syrup.

From: Bridges to Reading, Grades K-3: Teaching Reading Skills with Children's Literature. © 1999 Suzanne I. Barchers. Teacher Ideas Press (800) 237-6124.

Related books

Bayer, Jane. *A My Name Is Alice.* Illustrated by Steven Kellogg. New York: Trumpet, 1984.

Edwards, Pamela Duncan. *Some Smug Slug.* Illustrated by Henry Cole. New York: HarperCollins, 1996.

Gustafson, Scott. *Alphabet Soup: A Feast of Letters.* Shelton, Conn.: Greenwich Work-shop, 1990, 1994.

Walker, John. *Ridiculous Rhymes from A to Z.* Illustrated by David Catrow. New York: Henry Holt, 1995.

Yates, Gene. *The Elephant Alphabet Book.* Chicago: Kidsbooks, 1995.

From: Bridges to Reading, Grades K–3: Teaching Reading Skills with Children's Literature. © 1999 Suzanne I. Barchers. Teacher Ideas Press (800) 237-6124.

Wordplay: Homonyms

Rattigan, Jama Kim. *Truman's Aunt Farm.* Illustrated by G. Brian Karas. Boston: Houghton Mifflin, 1994.

Grade levels: K–1.

When Truman receives his birthday present from Aunt Fran, he expects to receive an ant farm. Instead, *aunts* begin to arrive at his home. They require a lot of work: feeding, entertaining, and so forth. Truman ends up with so many aunts he decides he has to find them their own nieces and nephews. Finally, another surprise arrives—his own Aunt Fran.

Activities

1. Read this book aloud, discussing the misunderstanding between the words *ant* and *aunt*. When did the students realize that the ant farm was not what Truman expected?

2. Ask the students if they can think of other words that sound alike but mean different things. Create a "Home for Homonyms" by developing a bulletin board that looks like the exterior of a house. As the students find examples of homonyms, they can affix them to the house. Try to fill up the house with homonyms.

3. Have the students create simple sentences that demonstrate their understanding of homonyms. For example:

   The bear isn't bare with all that fur on.
   I sent my sister one cent in the mail.

4. Discuss how homonyms can be difficult to distinguish. Give examples of ways to remember the different spellings. For example, the cent symbol is similar to the letter *c*, distinguishing it from the word *sent*.

Related books

Fowler, Allan. *Sound-A-Likes 1 One-Won!* Illustrated by Sue Cafferata. Lake Forest, Ill.: Forest House, 1996.

———. *Sound-A-Likes 2 Two-To-Too!* Illustrated by Sue Cafferata. Lake Forest, Ill.: Forest House, 1996.

Grover, Max. *Max's Wacky Taxi Day.* San Diego, Calif.: Harcourt Brace & Company, 1997.

Gwynne, Fred. *A Chocolate Moose for Dinner.* New York: Simon & Schuster, 1976.

———. *The King Who Rained.* New York: Simon & Schuster, 1970.

Klasky, Charles. *Rugs Have Naps (But Never Take Them).* Illustrated by Mike Venezia. Chicago: Childrens Press, 1984.

From: Bridges to Reading, Grades K–3: Teaching Reading Skills with Children's Literature. © 1999 Suzanne I. Barchers. Teacher Ideas Press (800) 237-6124.

From: Bridges to Reading, Grades K–3: Teaching Reading Skills with Children's Literature. © 1999 Suzanne I. Barchers. Teacher Ideas Press (800) 237-6124.

 Fowler, Allan. *Sound-A-Likes 1 One-Won!* Illustrated by Sue Cafferata. Lake Forest, Ill.: Forest House, 1996.

Grade levels: 2–3.

This collection of poetry features a pair of homonyms in each poem. The poems demonstrate the meanings of the homonyms, providing students with a way of remembering how to differentiate the words. This is an ideal book for introducing students to the study of homonyms.

Activities

1. Read the poems aloud. Discuss the differences in spelling. Is one word easier to remember because it is used more often? For example, *not* is a word that students learned very early to read and write. *Knot* may be one they didn't learn until they had been reading for a year or more.

2. Think about other words that could be used to create poems: *beau, bow; sent, cent, scent; chews, choose.* Consult Fry, Fountoukidis, and Polk's *The New Reading Teacher's Book of Lists* (see the "Related books" section below) for other examples. Have the students work in pairs to create new poems with the homonyms.

3. Create riddles that use homonyms for the punch line. Discuss how the homonym makes the joke work. For example:

   Was the boat very expensive?
   No, they had a sale (sail).

4. Declare a homonym day. Have the students share all the homonym poems and riddles they have found. Visit a younger class and try to stump the students with the riddles.

Related books

Fowler, Allan. *Sound-A-Likes 2 Two-To-Too!* Illustrated by Sue Cafferata. Lake Forest, Ill.: Forest House, 1996.

Fry, Edward Bernard, Dona Lee Fountoukidis, and Jacqueline Kress Polk. *The New Reading Teacher's Book of Lists.* Englewood Cliffs, N.J.: Prentice-Hall, 1985.

Gwynne, Fred. *A Chocolate Moose for Dinner.* New York: Simon & Schuster, 1976.

———. *The King Who Rained.* New York: Simon & Schuster, 1970.

Klasky, Charles. *Rugs Have Naps (But Never Take Them).* Illustrated by Mike Venezia. Chicago: Childrens Press, 1984.

Rattigan, Jama Kim. *Truman's Aunt Farm.* Illustrated by G. Brian Karas. Boston: Houghton Mifflin, 1994.

Wordplay: Onomatopoeia

 West, Colin. *"Buzz, Buzz, Buzz," Went Bumblebee.* Cambridge, Mass.: Candlewick Press, 1996.

Grade levels: K–1.

Bumblebee buzzed around, landing on many animals: a donkey, a rabbit, a cow, a crow, and a fox. Finally, he buzzed over to the butterfly, who asked if they could buzz around together.

Activities

1. Read aloud this short book to introduce the use of onomatopoeia through the word *buzz.* On the second reading, have the students chime in with *buzz* every time you come to it.

2. Ask the students if they can think of other words that sound like their meaning. Some words that start with *b* include *bang, beep, blip, boom, bong,* and *bowwow.*

3. Create a new version of the story by substituting the butterfly for the bee. Have the butterfly go "Flutter, flutter, flutter," and the animals respond with "Flutter off!" Write the new story on chart paper or use sticky notes to cover the word *buzz* with the word *flutter.* How do the changes affect the story?

4. Share several of the books listed in the "Related books" section below. Have the students find the examples of onomatopoeia in each of the books. In some, there may be only one example; therefore, the students will have to be very alert.

Related books

Baron, Alan. *Little Pig's Bouncy Ball.* Cambridge, Mass.: Candlewick Press, 1996.

———. *Red Fox Dances.* Cambridge, Mass.: Candlewick Press, 1996.

Benjamin, Alan. *Rat-a-Tat, Pitter Pat.* Photographs by Margaret Miller. New York: Thomas Y. Crowell, 1987.

Dodds, Dayle Ann. *Do Bunnies Talk?* Illustrated by A. Dubanevich. New York: HarperCollins, 1992.

Grossman, Bill. *The Banging Book.* Illustrated by Robert Zimmerman. New York: HarperCollins, 1995.

Root, Phyllis. *Mrs. Potter's Pig.* Illustrated by Russell Ayto. Cambridge, Mass.: Candlewick Press, 1996.

Schaefer, Carole Lexa. *The Squiggle.* Illustrated by Pierr Morgan. New York: Crown, 1996.

West, Colin. *One Day in the Jungle.* Cambridge, Mass.: Candlewick Press, 1995.

———. *"Only Joking!" Laughed the Lobster.* Cambridge, Mass.: Candlewick Press, 1995.

From: Bridges to Reading, Grades K–3: Teaching Reading Skills with Children's Literature. © 1999 Suzanne I. Barchers. Teacher Ideas Press (800) 237-6124.

From: Bridges to Reading, Grades K–3: Teaching Reading Skills with Children's Literature. © 1999 Suzanne I. Barchers. Teacher Ideas Press (800) 237-6124.

Schaefer, Carole Lexa. *The Squiggle.* Illustrated by Pierr Morgan. New York: Crown, 1996.

Grade levels: 2–3.

A little girl picks up a squiggle on the sidewalk. While she lags behind her classmates, she imagines it can be a dancing dragon, the Great Wall of China, the path of a circus acrobat, a trail of popping fireworks. Finally, she shows the class all the wonderful things she can do with the squiggle, and they join in the fun.

Activities

1. This charming story is full of onomatopoeia. Read it aloud. On the second reading, point out the use of onomatopoeia throughout. List examples on the board. Bring in some yarn or string. Have the students act out the story, using the yarn or string to make the squiggle.

2. Brainstorm a list of sound words from *A* to *Z*. The following list will help get you started: *argh, beep, chug, drip, eek, fizz, grind, hiss, icky, jiggle, konk, lisp, moo, neigh, ouch, plop, quack, roar, slurp, thump, vamoose, whack, yawn, zip.*

3. Have the students create their own series of shapes with the yarn. Perhaps the yarn becomes a zipper, duck, snake, or tugboat. Add the appropriate sound words. If possible, allow the students to glue down the yarn or string in the shape of their squiggles, adding the sound words below the shapes.

Related books

Baron, Alan. *Little Pig's Bouncy Ball.* Cambridge, Mass.: Candlewick Press, 1996.

———. *Red Fox Dances.* Cambridge, Mass.: Candlewick Press, 1996.

Benjamin, Alan. *Rat-a-Tat, Pitter Pat.* Photographs by Margaret Miller. New York: Thomas Y. Crowell, 1987.

Dodds, Dayle Ann. *Do Bunnies Talk?* Illustrated by A. Dubanevich. New York: HarperCollins, 1992.

Grossman, Bill. *The Banging Book.* Illustrated by Robert Zimmerman. New York: HarperCollins, 1995.

Root, Phyllis. *Mrs. Potter's Pig.* Illustrated by Russell Ayto. Cambridge, Mass.: Candlewick Press, 1996.

West, Colin. *"Buzz, Buzz, Buzz," Went Bumblebee.* Cambridge, Mass.: Candlewick Press, 1996.

———. *One Day in the Jungle.* Cambridge, Mass.: Candlewick Press, 1995.

———. *"Only Joking!" Laughed the Lobster.* Cambridge, Mass.: Candlewick Press, 1995.

Grover, Max. *Max's Wacky Taxi Day.* San Diego, Calif.: Harcourt Brace, 1997.

Grade levels: 2–3.

Max was ready to start his day when he noticed spring showers outside his window. Not the usual spring showers but a shower of metal springs! To make matters worse, the airport was socked in, inundated with colorful socks. A park bench had a park on it, and cars looked like car phones. This collection features colorful examples of word play.

Activities

1. Ask the students the following questions before reading the book:

    What is a spring shower?
    What is an airplane hangar?
    What happens when the airport is socked in?
    What is a seesaw?
    What is a tooth fairy?
    What does a park bench look like?

2. Then begin reading the book. Discuss how the words and images are used in this book. Explain that these are puns, using the illustrations to make the joke.

3. Begin to collect other examples of puns. Have the students illustrate them. Place them on a bulletin board with the heading *Very Punny!*

4. Share other books that have puns. Discuss how jokes often use puns, and encourage students to share those they have heard.

Related books

Bennett, Artie. *The Dinosaur Joke Book: A Compendium of Pre-Hysteric Puns.* Illustrated by Nate Evans. New York: Random House, 1998.

Gwynne, Fred. *A Chocolate Moose for Dinner.* New York: Simon & Schuster, 1976.

———. *The King Who Rained.* New York: Simon & Schuster, 1970.

Klasky, Charles. *Rugs Have Naps (But Never Take Them).* Illustrated by Mike Venezia. Chicago: Childrens Press, 1984.

From: Bridges to Reading, Grades K–3: Teaching Reading Skills with Children's Literature. © 1999 Suzanne I. Barchers. Teacher Ideas Press (800) 237-6124.

From: Bridges to Reading, Grades K–3: Teaching Reading Skills with Children's Literature. © 1999 Suzanne I. Barchers. Teacher Ideas Press (800) 237-6124.

Phillips, Louis. *Monster Riddles.* Illustrated by Arlene Dubanevich. New York: Penguin Putnam, 1998.

Grade levels: 2–3.

This collection of monster riddles will appeal to primary students. Discover what you get when you cross Godzilla with peanut butter, what a monster eats at a restaurant, how a monster counts to 23, and other amusing riddle "facts." The colorful illustrations enhance the jokes, adding to the absurd nature of the riddles.

Activities

1. Begin reading the book aloud, reading 10 or 15 riddles aloud while sharing the illustrations.

2. Read aloud more riddles without sharing the illustrations. Write each riddle and answer on the board. Have the students each choose a riddle to illustrate. Compile the illustrations into a book.

3. Choose another theme for writing riddles. Brainstorm a variety of ideas, for example, pickle riddles, dinosaur riddles, fish riddles, and chicken riddles. Suggest that the students use these riddles and modify them to function as new riddles. The following riddle is adapted from a monster riddle:

   What do you call an elephant that is 6 feet tall? Shorty.

4. Post a riddle a day. Have each student write a guess on a slip of paper and place each slip in a box or jar. Read the answers. Place all the correct answers in a jar and pull out a winner. Have that student choose a riddle for the next day. The student then reviews the answers and selects a winner for the next riddle.

Related books

Cole, Joanna, and Stephanie Calmenson. *The Laugh Book: A New Treasury of Humor for Children.* Illustrated by Marylin Hafner. Garden City, N.Y.: Doubleday, 1986, 1987.

Lewis, J. Patrick. *Riddle-icious.* Illustrated by Debbie Tilley. New York: Alfred A. Knopf, 1996.

Terban, Marvin. *Funny You Should Ask: How to Make Up Jokes and Riddles with Wordplay.* Illustrated by John O'Brien. New York: Clarion, 1992.

Maestro, Betsy, and Giulio Maestro. *All Aboard Overnight: A Book of Compound Words.* New York: Clarion, 1992.

Grade levels: 2–3.

A little girl and her mother take a train *overnight.* On the way they do some *sightseeing,* take *snapshots,* and enjoy the *sunshine.* Many other compound words are integrated into this story and made clear through boldfacing. The simple story allows the reader to focus on the natural usage of many compound words.

Activities

1. Before reading the story, ask if any of the students have ridden on a train. Ask them what they saw on the ride. Then discuss all the things they might see if they were to take a train ride. List these things on the board.

2. Read the book aloud. Then tell the students that all the boldfaced words in the story are compound words, words made up of two other words. Read the story again and have the students raise their hands every time they hear a compound word.

3. Write the compound words on the board. Did the students predict any of the words in the earlier discussion about what they might see on a train ride? Discuss how the words were created.

4. If possible, share Cynthia Basil's *Breakfast in the Afternoon* (see the "Related books" section below). This source provides a variety of compound words. Alternatively, use any picture dictionary to generate a list of compound words. Work with the class to create another story that uses a variety of compound words. For example, a story about a trip on a river offers many possibilities: *rowboat, sailboat, waterwheel, paddleboat, riverboat, boathouse, houseboat, speedboat, lighthouse, shoreline.*

Related book

Basil, Cynthia. *Breakfast in the Afternoon.* Illustrated by Janet McCaffery. New York: Morrow, 1979.

Clements, Andrew. *Double Trouble in Walla Walla.* Illustrated by Salvatore Murdocca. Brookfield, Conn.: Millbrook Press, 1997.

From: Bridges to Reading, Grades K-3: Teaching Reading Skills with Children's Literature. © 1999 Suzanne I. Barchers. Teacher Ideas Press (800) 237-6124.

From: Bridges to Reading, Grades K-3: Teaching Reading Skills with Children's Literature. © 1999 Suzanne I. Barchers. Teacher Ideas Press (800) 237-6124.

Egielski, Richard. *Buz.* New York: HarperCollins, 1995.

Grade levels: K–1.

A young boy swallows a bug along with his cornflakes. Buz tries to escape, but he can't get out of the boy's body. The boy goes to the doctor, who gives him some pills. The pills chase Buz, who finally escapes out the boy's ear and into the bathtub. However, Buz is so exhausted he goes to his own doctor, who diagnoses that he has a germ.

Activities

1. Before reading, ask the students what a bug is. They may offer many suggestions: an insect, a computer bug or virus, a germ. Accept all suggestions, writing them on the board.

2. Read the book aloud. After the first reading, tell the students to listen for each time you read the words *bug* and *Buz.* Ask them to raise their hands each time they hear them. How many times do they hear a word beginning with the letter *b?*

3. Discuss how the author made up a fanciful bug in the story. Give the students paper and crayons or markers. Have the students create their own bug. Have the students copy the word *bug* onto their paper.

4. Compile the illustrations into a *Bug* book. If available, have the students refer to books about bugs, such as Sandra Markle's *Creepy, Crawly Baby Bugs* (see the "Related books" section below).

5. If time allows, create a follow-up to the story. How will Buz get rid of the germ if the pills don't work? How does the germ feel trapped inside a bug?

Related books

Baron, Alan. *Little Pig's Bouncy Ball.* Cambridge, Mass.: Candlewick Press, 1996.

Bottner, Barbara. *Bootsie Barker Bites.* Illustrated by Peggy Rathmann. New York: Putnam, 1992.

Henkes, Kevin. *The Biggest Boy.* Illustrated by Nancy Tafuri. New York: Morrow, 1995.

Kraus, Robert. *Little Louie the Baby Bloomer.* Illustrated by Jose Aruego and Ariane Dewey. New York: HarperCollins, 1998.

Markle, Sandra. *Creepy, Crawly Baby Bugs.* New York: Walker, 1996.

West, Colin. *"Buzz, Buzz, Buzz," Went Bumblebee.* Cambridge, Mass.: Candlewick Press, 1996.

Henkes, Kevin. *Circle Dogs.* Illustrated by Dan Yaccarino. New York: Greenwillow, 1998.

Grade levels: K–1.

Two circle dogs live in a square house. They curl up in the shape of circles to sleep, but stretch out when it's time to wake and play. They eat out of circle bowls, play a bit, and then sleep some more. When someone comes to the door, they wake and bark. But when nighttime comes, they curl up in circles again.

Activities

1. Review the names of the shapes. Ask the students which shape starts with the letter *c*. Discuss the sound of *c* as contrasted with the sound of *c* in the word *cat*.

2. Have the students draw the letter *c* on a piece of paper. Discuss how the letter looks like an incomplete circle.

3. Read aloud the story. During the second reading, have the students identify as many shapes as they can. Make a list of them while you read. For example, the list may begin like the example below.

4. Have the students make an illustrated list of all the items they can think of that are circle shaped. They might include wheels, pizzas, and rings.

Squares	Circles	Triangles	Rectangles
House	Dogs	Dog's ears	House's door
House's windows	Sun		Mail
Yard	Alarm clock		

Related book

Hoban, Tana. *So Many Circles, So Many Squares.* New York: Greenwillow, 1998.

From: Bridges to Reading, Grades K–3: Teaching Reading Skills with Children's Literature. © 1999 Suzanne I. Barchers. Teacher Ideas Press (800) 237-6124.

Karlin, Nurit. *The Fat Cat Sat on the Mat.* New York: HarperCollins, 1996.

Grade levels: K–1.

Wilma the Witch has a fat cat. When it sits on the rat's mat, the rat becomes angry. Of course, the cat will not get off the mat, in spite of the bat and hat, who implore him to leave. When Wilma's broom sweeps in the window, they all end up on the mat until Wilma returns. Everything returns to normal, to the relief of the mat. Although simple and predictable, the zany story makes this an amusing book to read.

Activities

1. Write the word *cat* on the board. Ask the students to identify it. Help them sound it out if necessary, explaining that the *c* sound is called a hard sound. Compare it with the sound of *c* at the beginning of the word *circle*.

2. Ask the students to think of all the words they can think of that rhyme with *cat*. Make a list on the board. If they have trouble with rhyming words, write the word *at* on the board a number of times. Then begin with the letter *b* and proceed through the alphabet, recording the examples that are truly words. Tell the students that these words all belong to the *at* family.

3. Read the book aloud. When finished, look at the list of rhyming words. How many were in the story?

4. Read the book again, telling students that this time you want them to read the word *cat* every time you come to it. If appropriate, tell the students that usually when *c* comes before the letters *a, o,* and *u,* it will have this sound. When *c* comes before the letters *e* and *i,* it will have the beginning sound of the word *circle*.

Related books

Jeram, Anita. *Contrary Mary.* Cambridge, Mass.: Candlewick Press, 1995.

McBratney, Sam. *The Caterpillow Fight.* Illustrated by Jill Barton. Cambridge, Mass.: Candlewick Press, 1996.

Root, Phyllis. *Contrary Bear.* Illustrated by Laura Cornell. New York: HarperCollins, 1996.

From: Bridges to Reading, Grades K–3: Teaching Reading Skills with Children's Literature. © 1999 Suzanne I. Barchers. Teacher Ideas Press (800) 237-6124.

Word Recognition: Consonant *d*

Jeram, Anita. *Daisy Dare*. Cambridge, Mass.: Candlewick Press, 1995.

Grade levels: K–1.

Daisy Dare, a little mouse, loves to do daring things. She boasts to her friends that nothing scares her. She walks along a wall and even eats a worm! When her friends dare her to take the bell off the cat's collar, she finally gets scared. But she accepts the dare and succeeds by just a whisker!

Activities

1. Ask the students if they have ever been challenged to accept a dare. Ask them to share the scariest things they have done.

2. Read the book aloud. Discuss how dares can sometimes get a person in trouble.

3. Write the words *Daisy Dare* on the board. Ask the students with what letter each of these words begins. Can they think of other words that begin with the letter *d?* Write the words on the board.

4. Read the story again. Can the students find other words that start with the letter *d?*

5. Brainstorm other story titles about Daisy that use words that start with the letter *d*. Examples might include:

   Daisy Dives
   Daisy Decides
   Daisy Dillydallies
   Daisy Dances

   Create new stories about Daisy that use a variety of words that start with *d.*

Related books

Fanelli, Sara. *Doggy Book*. Philadelphia: Running Press, 1998.

Hurd, Thacher. *Art Dog*. New York: HarperCollins, 1996.

From: Bridges to Reading, Grades K–3: Teaching Reading Skills with Children's Literature. © 1999 Suzanne I. Barchers. Teacher Ideas Press (800) 237-6124.

From: Bridges to Reading, Grades K–3: Teaching Reading Skills with Children's Literature. © 1999 Suzanne I. Barchers. Teacher Ideas Press (800) 237-6124.

Lionni, Leo. *Fish Is Fish.* New York: Random House, 1970.

Grade levels: K–1.

A tadpole and a minnow are great friends. The minnow is distraught at the thought of the tadpole turning into a frog. Finally, the tadpole becomes a frog and hops away to see the world. On his return he tells the minnow, now a fully grown fish, about the wonderful things he has seen. The fish is eager to see the world and leaps out of the water. Fortunately, the frog pushes him back into the water, where he decides to stay.

Activities

1. Write the word *fish* on the board. Ask the students what they know about fish. Discuss their body parts, such as gills, scales, and fins. Then discuss their living environment and how they need water to survive. Tell students that *fish* begins with the letter *f* and ask them to think of other words that start with *f*.

2. Read the book aloud. Ask the students what other creatures' names began with the letter *f*. Write the word *frog* next to the word *fish*.

3. Discuss how the fish interpreted the frog's descriptions of things he saw as if they were all fish involved in the activity. Give students various colors of construction paper, along with large sheets of light blue paper. Have the students cut out from the construction paper and glue onto the light blue paper imaginative fish designs. Have them write the word *fish* on the bottom of the page. Display them in the classroom.

4. Bring in a fishbowl. Tell the students to write all the words they can think of that start with the letter *f* on small fish-shaped pieces of paper. Have them place them in the fishbowl for display in the classroom.

Related books

Baron, Alan. *Red Fox Dances.* Cambridge, Mass.: Candlewick Press, 1996.

Edwards, Pamela Duncan. *Four Famished Foxes and Fosdyke.* Illustrated by Henry Cole. New York: HarperCollins, 1995.

Egielski, Richard. *The Gingerbread Boy.* New York: HarperCollins, 1997.

Grade levels: K–1.

In this urban version of a traditional story, a woman bakes a gingerbread boy. He jumps out the window and begins to run through the city. He escapes a rat, some construction workers, some musicians, and a police officer. When he comes to a lake, he lets a fox carry him across on his shoulders. Finally, he crawls on the fox's nose, and the fox flips him into the air and neatly eats him.

Activities

1. Hold up the book. Ask the students if they can read the title of the story. Write the word *gingerbread* on the board and discuss how it begins and the sound the letter *g* makes in this word. Contrast it with the sound the letter *g* makes in a word such as *go* or *good.*

2. Read the story aloud. Then read a version of the story that has a more traditional setting. Contrast the settings, discussing the differences.

3. On the second reading, invite the students to join you in the refrain, "Run run run as fast as you can. . . ." Discuss why the refrain ends with the word *man* instead of *boy* (to rhyme).

4. Brainstorm other settings in which the story could take place. Perhaps the Gingerbread Boy could live near a zoo, in the desert, or on a mountain. Rewrite the story to fit the new setting. Consider writing what a gingerbread *girl* might do.

5. Use the recipe provided in the book to create gingerbread boys and girls for the students to decorate and eat. If possible, visit a bakery that makes gingerbread boys.

Related books

Cook, Scott. *The Gingerbread Boy.* New York: Alfred A. Knopf, 1987.

Kimmel, Eric A. *The Gingerbread Man.* Illustrated by Megan Lloyd. New York: Holiday House, 1993.

Pomerantz, Charlotte. *Whiff, Sniff, Nibble and Chew: The Gingerbread Boy.* Illustrated by Monica Incisa. New York: Greenwillow, 1984.

From: *Bridges to Reading, Grades K–3: Teaching Reading Skills with Children's Literature.* © 1999 Suzanne I. Barchers. Teacher Ideas Press (800) 237-6124.

From: Bridges to Reading, Grades K–3: Teaching Reading Skills with Children's Literature. © 1999 Suzanne I. Barchers. Teacher Ideas Press (800) 237-6124.

Brown, Margaret Wise. *Goodnight Moon.* Illustrated by Clement Hurd. New York: Harper & Row, 1947.

Grade levels: K–1.

A baby rabbit goes to bed in a room with kittens, mittens, a bowl of mush, and other things. The rabbit bids goodnight to a variety of items: the moon, a cow, a light, a red balloon, the chairs. This comforting book has endured as the ideal going-to-sleep book.

Activities

1. Show the students the book. How many of them know it? Write the word *goodnight* on the board. Ask the students what two words are in this big (compound) word. Discuss how *good* begins with the letter *g*. Compare its sound with the sound of the letter *g* in *gingerbread* (see page 160).

2. Read the book aloud, inviting the students to read the story with you.

3. Write a new version of the book, using the items in the classroom. Brainstorm all the things that could be told goodnight: blackboard, desks, chairs, chalk, books. Structure the story in a similar fashion, emphasizing the word *goodnight.*

4. Have the students go home that night and make a list of all the things that they could say goodnight to in their rooms. The list might start like the following:

   Goodnight bed.
   Goodnight stuffed bear.
   Goodnight schoolbooks.

   Have the students bring their lists to class to share.

Related books

Aliki. *Hello! Good-bye!* New York: Greenwillow, 1996.

Brown, Margaret Wise. *A Child's Good Morning Book.* Illustrated by Jean Charlot. New York: HarperCollins, 1995.

Kelly, Sean. *Boom Baby Moon.* Illustrated by Ron Hauge. New York: Dell, 1993.

Word Recognition: Consonant *h*

Aliki. *Hello! Good-bye!* New York: Greenwillow, 1996.

Grade levels: K–1.

The first section of this book emphasizes the word *hello.* The author describes the use of hello as an introduction, welcome, and greeting in a variety of other ways, such as *yoo-hoo!* Nonverbal greetings, the meanings of greetings in other languages, and the uses of greetings are explored. The second half of the book discusses the use of the word *good-bye.*

Activities

1. When the students enter the classroom that morning, greet each one with a handshake while saying *hello.*

2. Before reading the first half of the book aloud, remind the students of their greeting that day. Write the word *hello* on the board. Ask the students to tell you all the ways someone might greet another person. Write all the ideas on the board. Discuss how *hello* starts with the letter *h.*

3. Read the book aloud. Before reading the first half a second time, tell the students to listen for other greetings that include words that begin with the letter *h: howdy, yoo-hoo, hug, your health, happy landing, have a good day.*

4. Research other languages and their greetings. Do other languages have words for greetings that start with the letter *h?*

5. Give the students paper and pencils. Have them trace around their hands. Write the word *hand* beneath the drawing. Write all the words for greetings that begin with the letter *h* inside the outline of the hand.

Related books

Hoberman, Mary Ann. *A House Is a House for Me.* Illustrated by Betty Fraser. New York: Viking, 1978.

Rosen, Michael. *This Is Our House.* Illustrated by Bob Graham. Cambridge, Mass.: Candlewick Press, 1996.

From: Bridges to Reading, Grades K–3: Teaching Reading Skills with Children's Literature. © 1999 Suzanne I. Barchers. Teacher Ideas Press (800) 237-6124.

West, Colin. *"Only Joking!" Laughed the Lobster.* Cambridge, Mass.: Candlewick Press, 1995.

Grade levels: K–1.

Lobster, a practical joker, first tells Fish that a shark is following him. When Fish becomes alarmed, the lobster tells him he is only joking. He repeats the prank with Eel, Crab, Turtle, and Octopus. Finally, a shark confronts him, and the lobster finds that the shark is *not* joking when he swallows him!

Activities

1. Write the word *joke* on the board. Ask the students what it means to play a practical joke on someone. Ask the students to identify the first letter in the word *joke.* Read aloud or tell the fable "The Boy Who Cried Wolf" and discuss what happens to the boy because of his repeated false alarms.

2. Next, write the words *"Only joking!"* on the board. Have the students read it and watch for it as you read the book aloud.

3. On the second reading, have the students read aloud the words *only joking* with you each time you come to them.

4. Brainstorm additional sea creatures that the lobster could trick. For example, he might trick a dolphin, shrimp, jellyfish, or ray. Then expand the story to include the other sea creatures, until the lobster is finally swallowed by the shark.

5. For another variation, think of wild animals that could be used in the same story format. For example, a monkey might repeatedly tell jungle animals that a lion is behind them, until the monkey is eaten by a lion.

Related books

Fine, John Christopher. *Big Stuff in the Ocean.* Golden, Colo.: Fulcrum, 1998.

Pallota, Jerry. *The Underwater Alphabet Book.* Illustrated by Edgar Stewart. New York: Trumpet, 1991.

Waddell, Martin. *John Joe and the Big Hen.* Illustrated by Paul Howard. Cambridge, Mass.: Candlewick Press, 1995.

West, Colin. *One Day in the Jungle.* Cambridge, Mass.: Candlewick Press, 1995.

From: Bridges to Reading, Grades K–3: Teaching Reading Skills with Children's Literature. © 1999 Suzanne I. Barchers. Teacher Ideas Press (800) 237-6124.

Hulme, Joy N. *Counting by Kangaroos.* Illustrated by Betsy Scheld. New York: W. H. Freeman, 1995.

Grade levels: K–1.

Three kangaroos show up at Sue and Fae's house. Sue and Fae invite them to stay for a visit. But then a variety of Australian animals crawl out of the kangaroos' pockets. Soon, squirrel gliders, koalas, bandicoots, wombats, quokkas, numbats, echnidas, and wallabies fill the house. There's only one thing left to do—start a zoo!

Activities

1. Write the word *kangaroo* on the board. Ask the students to identify it and help them figure out the meaning of the word, if necessary. Discuss how the word starts with the letter *k*. Ask them to think of other words that begin with the letter *k*, for example, *king, kite, key, kayak, kitten.*

2. Read the book aloud. Discuss the many animals that the kangaroos carried in their pockets. Is such a scenario realistic? Read informational books about kangaroos to learn how they carry their young in their pockets. Discuss the animals that are described in this book on the first page.

3. Can the students think of other creatures that start with the letter *k: katydid, killdeer plover, kinkajou, koodoo, koala.* Look up in a dictionary any creatures with which they are unfamiliar.

4. Make a bulletin board of a kangaroo. Give it a pocket that can be used for storing words. Have students write all the words they can think of that start with the letter *k* and place them in the kangaroo's pocket. Continue adding to the pocket over the course of a week or two.

Related books

Murphy, Stuart J. *Too Many Kangaroo Things to Do!* Illustrated by Kevin O'Malley. New York: HarperCollins, 1996.

Payne, Emmy. *Katy No-Pocket.* Illustrated by Hans Augusto Rey. Boston: Houghton Mifflin, 1944.

From: Bridges to Reading, Grades K–3: Teaching Reading Skills with Children's Literature. © 1999 Suzanne I. Barchers. Teacher Ideas Press (800) 237-6124.

From: Bridges to Reading, Grades K–3: Teaching Reading Skills with Children's Literature. © 1999 Suzanne I. Barchers. Teacher Ideas Press (800) 237-6124.

Greenfield, Eloise. *Honey, I Love.* Illustrated by Jan Spivey Gilchrist. New York: HarperCollins, 1978, 1995.

Grade levels: K–1.

With gentle rhymes, a little girl shares what she loves. She loves her cousin from the South, a flying pool (water hose), playing dolls with her friend, going on a ride, and her mother's arm. She does *not* love going to sleep, of course! This charming book ends with the declaration that she loves herself as well.

Activities

1. Write the word *love* on the board. Ask the students what they think of when they see that word. Brainstorm a variety of words that begin with the letter *l* and write them on the board.

2. Read the book aloud. Next, have the students tell you all the things the little girl loves. Write those on the board.

3. Give each student a large piece of white paper. Have them use a red crayon or marker to draw a large heart in the center of the paper. Brainstorm things they love that start with the letter *l*. Examples might include *lollipops, luck, letters, libraries, life, leaves,* and *learning.* Have each student write words that start with the letter *l* that they love in the heart. Write "What I Love" above the heart.

4. Next, brainstorm things that start with the letter *l* that they don't love. Examples might include *laundry, lists, laziness, loans, lice, lightning,* and *limping.* Have the students make another list with the heading "What I Don't Love."

Related books

Carlson, Nancy. *I Like Me!* New York: Trumpet, 1988.

Joosse, Barbara M. *Mama, Do You Love Me?* Illustrated by Barbara Lavallee. San Francisco: Chronicle, 1991.

Marshall, Edward. *Fox in Love.* Illustrated by James Marshall. New York: Dial, 1982.

Rosenberg, Liz. *Monster Mama.* Illustrated by Stephen Gammell. New York: Putnam, 1993.

Grade levels: K–1.

Patrick Edward's mother is a monster. Although she frightens people in the neighborhood, she is loving and kind to Patrick. One day, three boys chase Patrick Edward, tie him to a tree, and ridicule his mother. He roars at them, breaking free and chasing them down the hill. His mother comes out of her cave and takes the boys back to their home, where they all reconcile and have dessert together.

Activities

1. Write the word *monster* on the board. Ask the students to identify the word. What do they think of when they read or hear the word *monster?* Discuss all the different kinds of monsters they see in the movies or read about in books.

2. Discuss how the word *monster* begins with the letter *m.* Write the word *mama* on the board. Ask the students to identify the letters used in the word. Discuss the sound of the letter *m* in *mama.* Explain that this story is about a very unusual monster.

3. Read the story aloud, allowing the students time to enjoy the illustrations. Discuss the unusual use of paint in the illustrations. Next, brainstorm people or objects that begin with the letter *m.* Examples might include *mom, mop, man, muffin,* and *minnow.*

4. Have the students use watercolors to paint a picture of something that begins with the letter *m.* Then set up a paint center. Rest a piece of fine screen at least 9 x 12 inches in size across four strips of wood. Mix up several colors of tempera paint to medium thickness. Provide a toothbrush for each color of paint. Each student can then place the watercolor drawing under the screen, dip a brush in the paint, and rub the brush across the screen. This will cause a splatter effect similar to the one in the book.

Related books

Caseley, Judith. *Mama, Coming and Going.* New York: Greenwillow, 1994.

Ford, Miela. *Mom and Me.* New York: Greenwillow, 1998.

Novak, Matt. *Mouse TV.* New York: Orchard, 1994.

Ziefert, Harriet, and Simms Taback. *Who Said Moo?* New York: HarperCollins, 1996.

From: Bridges to Reading, Grades K-3: Teaching Reading Skills with Children's Literature. © 1999 Suzanne I. Barchers. Teacher Ideas Press (800) 237-6124.

From: Bridges to Reading, Grades K–3: Teaching Reading Skills with Children's Literature. © 1999 Suzanne I. Barchers. Teacher Ideas Press (800) 237-6124.

Murphy, Jill. *The Last Noo-Noo.* Cambridge, Mass.: Candlewick Press, 1995.

Grade levels: K–1.

Marlon's granny declares that he is too old for a pacifier. He tells her the pacifier is called a *noo-noo*. His mother agrees that perhaps it's time to get rid of the noo-noo, and she gathers them all up for the garbage. But Marlon has noo-noos hidden all over the house. When other monsters try to snatch his next-to-the-last noo-noo, a fierce tug-of-war ensues, and his noo-noo lands in the lake. Marlon is prepared, however. He has planted his last one—to grow a noo-noo tree.

Activities

1. Write the word *noo-noo* on the board. Talk about the sounds of the letters as the students figure out the word. Tell the students that *noo-noo* is a made-up word and ask them if they can guess what it means.

2. Read the story aloud. Did the students predict the meaning of *noo-noo?* Did any of them have special words for pacifiers, such as *binky* or *lovey?* Were their names contrived as well? Did they have a special blanket or toy instead of a pacifier?

3. Discuss how such items from childhood can be comforting, especially when going to sleep.

4. Brainstorm other words that begin with the letters *no* and write them on the board. Examples might include *nobody, nod, noise, none, noon, normal, north, nose, note, notice, not,* and *now.*

5. Create a bulletin board with a tree shape. Label it *The N Tree.* Have the students write all the words they can think of that start with the letter *n* on leaves and add them to the tree. Continue to add leaves as the students discover more words.

Related books

Hayes, Sarah. *Nine Ducks Nine.* Cambridge, Mass.: Candlewick Press, 1990.

Wood, Audrey. *The Napping House.* Illustrated by Don Wood. San Diego, Calif.: Harcourt Brace & Company, 1984.

Word Recognition: Consonant *p*

Hutchins, Pat. *Little Pink Pig.* New York: Greenwillow, 1994.

Grade levels: K–1.

Little Pink Pig's mother searches diligently for Little Pink Pig. Every time she calls for him, Little Pink Pig doesn't hear her. When she leaves to ask the animals where he is, Little Pink Pig squeals for her to wait, but she doesn't hear him! While visiting a variety of animals, Little Pink Pig gets into various predicaments. Finally, all the animals call together, and Little Pink Pig hears them.

Activities

1. Write the words *Little Pink Pig* on the board. Ask the students to read the words. Help them identify the words, discussing how the words are capitalized because they are used as a name of the main character in the story.

2. Read the story aloud. Discuss how *pink* and *pig* begin with the letter *p*.

3. Make a list of all the animals in the book. Then list their corresponding sounds. The example below begins the process.

4. Reread the book. Discuss the troubles Little Pink Pig has throughout the story and why he and his mother can't hear each other. Add a third column to the chart labeled *Little Pink Pig's Predicaments*. Discuss what the word *predicament* means and how it starts with the letter *p*. List the various predicaments Little Pink Pig encounters with each corresponding animal.

5. Think of words related to a farm that begin with the letter *p*. Examples might include *pen, pigsty, plow, peas,* and *pumpkin*.

Little Pink Pig's mother	oink
Little Pink Pig	squeal
Horse	neigh
Cow	moo

From: Bridges to Reading, Grades K–3: Teaching Reading Skills with Children's Literature. © 1999 Suzanne I. Barchers. Teacher Ideas Press (800) 237-6124.

From: Bridges to Reading, Grades K-3: Teaching Reading Skills with Children's Literature. © 1999 Suzanne I. Barchers. Teacher Ideas Press (800) 237-6124.

Related books

Delaney, A. *Pearl's First Prize Plant.* New York: HarperCollins, 1997.

Henkes, Kevin. *Lilly's Purple Plastic Purse.* New York: Greenwillow, 1996.

MacDonald, Margaret Read. *Pickin' Peas.* Illustrated by Pat Cummings. New York: HarperCollins, 1998.

McPhail, David. *Pigs Ahoy.* New York: Dutton, 1995.

Kuskin, Karla. *Patchwork Island.* Illustrated by Petra Mathers. New York: HarperCollins, 1994.

Grade levels: K–1.

A mother stitches up a quilt while a youngster plays. She sews in green for leaves and fields, blue for the water, and red and brown for the road. When finished, she tells the youngster that she can play on the quilt during the day and use it as a cover during the cold nights on the island.

Activities

1. Bring in a quilt and display it in the classroom. Ask the students to describe any quilts they have at home. Have them bring in quilts to share, if possible. Write the word *quilt* on the board. Explain to the students that the letter *q* is almost always followed by the letter *u.*

2. Ask the students if they can think of other words that start with the letter *q: queen, quack, quail, quill, quick, question, quit, quiz, quiet.*

3. Read the book aloud. Discuss that the quilt in this story is a patchwork quilt. Refer to the various quilts in Ann Whitford Paul's *Eight Hands Round: A Patchwork Alphabet* (see the "Related books" section below).

4. Give each student a cloth square and an indelible marker, and have him or her write a word that begins with the letter *q* or draw a picture of a word that begins with *q* on the square. Let each student sew the square to the others or have a volunteer parent piece them together to form a quilt. Display the quilt as a record of words that begin with the letter *q.*

Related books

Johnston, Tony. *The Quilt Story.* Illustrated by Tomie dePaola. New York: Putnam, 1984.

Jonas, Ann. *The Quilt.* New York: Greenwillow, 1984.

Paul, Ann Whitford. *Eight Hands Round: A Patchwork Alphabet.* Illustrated by Jeanette Winter. New York: HarperCollins, 1991.

Willard, Nancy. *The Mountains of Quilt.* Illustrated by Tomie dePaola. San Diego, Calif.: Harcourt Brace Jovanovich, 1987.

From: Bridges to Reading, Grades K–3: Teaching Reading Skills with Children's Literature. © 1999 Suzanne I. Barchers. Teacher Ideas Press (800) 237-6124.

From: Bridges to Reading, Grades K-3: Teaching Reading Skills with Children's Literature. © 1999 Suzanne I. Barchers. Teacher Ideas Press (800) 237-6124.

Gantos, Jack, and Nicole Rubel. *Back to School for Rotten Ralph.* New York: HarperCollins, 1998.

Grade levels: K–1.

Sarah looks forward to going back to school, but Rotten Ralph, her cat, doesn't want her to go. He plays endless tricks on her, trying to get her to stay home. Rotten Ralph follows her to school, dressed up as a student. There, he continues to play tricks on her, and she doesn't make any new friends. Finally Ralph is discovered, but because everyone at school loves cats, they all become Sarah's friends. When they go home, Sarah tells Ralph he'll always be her best friend.

Activities

1. Hold up the cover of the book. Do the students know other Rotten Ralph stories? Write the words *Rotten Ralph* on the board and help the students read them aloud. Discuss how both words start with the letter *r*.

2. Ask the students why they think Ralph got the name *Rotten*. What could he do that would be problematic at school?

3. Read the book aloud. When finished, create a chart of all of Rotten Ralph's rotten tricks. Use the example below as a starting point.

4. Discuss why Rotten Ralph did so many tricks. Were they necessary?

Rotten Ralph's trick #1	Rotten Ralph squirts Sarah.
Rotten Ralph's trick #2	Rotten Ralph takes Sarah's book bag.
Rotten Ralph's trick #3	Rotten Ralph breaks Sarah's pencil points.
Rotten Ralph's trick #4	Rotten Ralph turns back the hands on the alarm clock.

Word Recognition: Consonant *r*

Related books

Baron, Alan. *Red Fox Dances.* Cambridge, Mass.: Candlewick Press, 1996.

Gantos, Jack, and Nicole Rubel. *Rotten Ralph's Show and Tell.* Boston: Houghton Mifflin, 1989.

Peek, Merle. *Roll Over! A Counting Song.* New York: Clarion, 1981.

From: Bridges to Reading, Grades K-3: Teaching Reading Skills with Children's Literature. © 1999 Suzanne I. Barchers. Teacher Ideas Press (800) 237-6124.

From: Bridges to Reading, Grades K–3: Teaching Reading Skills with Children's Literature. © 1999 Suzanne I. Barchers. Teacher Ideas Press (800) 237-6124.

Marzolla, Jean. *Sun Song.* Illustrated by Laura Regan. New York: HarperCollins, 1995.

Grade levels: K–1.

This book celebrates the role the sun plays in everyone's lives, from animals to flowers to humans. The day begins with the sun shining on a newborn fawn and then moves to, among other things, a water hole, a farm, a robin's nest, and a boy and his dog. The role of the sun in nurturing life is gently emphasized right through to the end of the day.

Activities

1. Ask the students to identify the word *sun*. Have them tell you everything they know about the sun.

2. Read the book aloud, taking time to enjoy the striking illustrations.

3. On the second reading, tell the students that they are to listen for all the words that begin with the letter *s*. Write the words on the board.

4. Brainstorm other words that begin with the letter *s*. Examples might include *sack, saddle, sail, salt, sailor, salamander, sandals, sand, sardines, satellite, saw, scarf,* and *spider*. Encourage the students to look in easy dictionaries for additional examples.

5. Give each student a large piece of yellow paper. Have them draw a large circle in the upper half of the page. On the lower half of the page, have them write the following sentence:

    The sun shines down on the _____.

    Have each student choose a word that begins with the letter *s* to write in the blank. Then have the students illustrate the item.

Related books

Edwards, Richard. *Something's Coming.* Illustrated by Dana Kubick. Cambridge, Mass.: Candlewick Press, 1995.

Millen, C. M. *A Symphony for the Sheep.* Illustrated by Mary Azarian. Boston: Houghton Mifflin, 1996.

Shaw, Nancy. *Sheep on a Ship.* Illustrated by Margot Apple. Boston: Houghton Mifflin, 1989.

———. *Sheep Out to Eat.* Illustrated by Margot Apple. Boston: Houghton Mifflin, 1992.

Word Recognition: Consonant *t*

Tchana, Katrin Hyman, and Louise Tchana Pami. *Oh, No, Toto!* Illustrated by Colin Bootman. New York: Scholastic, 1997.

Grade levels: K–1.

In Cameroon, West Africa, where Toto lives, *Toto Gourmand* means "Toto, the Hungry One." Toto goes to the market with his grandmother, promising to behave. He wants a puffpuff but manages to spill the entire tray. Next, he swipes a hard-boiled egg. Soon he has gotten into so much trouble that Big Mami takes him home. But even when he gets home, he can't resist eating an entire pot of soup!

Activities

1. Write the word *Toto* on the board. Ask the students to read it aloud, discussing the meaning and how it uses the letter *t* twice.

2. Read the story aloud, taking time to enjoy the colorful illustrations. Discuss the marketplace and all the unusual foods described. Find Cameroon on the globe or on a world map. Reread the story and have the students join in every time someone says, "Oh, no, Toto!"

3. Make a chart that lists all of Toto's troubles, using the one below as an example.

4. Use the glossary to explore the Cameroonian foods described in the story. If possible, find a recipe for one of the foods and make it in class, following all safety precautions.

Toto's first trouble	Toto spilled the puffpuffs.
Toto's second trouble	Toto swiped a hard-boiled egg.
Toto's third trouble	Toto fell in a tub of palm oil.
Toto's fourth trouble	Toto ate the *koki* and cassava stick.

Related books

Gershator, Phillis. *Tukama Tootles the Flute.* Illustrated by Synthia Saint James. New York: Orchard, 1994.

Soto, Gary. *Too Many Tamales.* Illustrated by Ed Martinez. New York: G. P. Putnam's Sons, 1993.

174

From: Bridges to Reading, Grades K–3: Teaching Reading Skills with Children's Literature. © 1999 Suzanne I. Barchers. Teacher Ideas Press (800) 237-6124.

From: Bridges to Reading, Grades K–3: Teaching Reading Skills with Children's Literature. © 1999 Suzanne I. Barchers. Teacher Ideas Press (800) 237-6124.

Carle, Eric. *The Very Busy Spider.* New York: Philomel, 1985.

Grade levels: K–1.

The spider begins to spin her web early one morning. The horse asks her to go for a ride, but she is very busy spinning her web. The cow, sheep, goat, pig, dog, cat, duck, and rooster all try to engage her in an activity. Finally, she finishes her web and catches a fly!

Activities

1. Write the word *very* on the board. Ask the students to think of words they could use *very* with: *very hungry, very sleepy, very quiet, very happy.* Discuss how the word *very* begins with the letter *v.* If the students contribute *very busy,* tell them that the book is about an insect that is very busy.

2. Read the book aloud. On the second reading, invite the students to read aloud with you the repeated sentence about the spider, emphasizing the words *very busy.*

3. Brainstorm other farm animals that might ask the spider to do something. For example, perhaps a chicken could ask the spider to watch her hatch an egg. Write additional lines to expand the story.

4. Return to the beginning of the book. Page through the pictures and ask the students to find the fly on the pages.

5. Point out how the web is developed on the pages. Pass the book around so the students can feel the raised web.

6. During the next few days create a "Very Busy" list. List all the times you can apply the word *very* to something the students are doing and add them to the list: *very silly, very quiet, very smart, very helpful.*

Related books

Carle, Eric. *The Very Hungry Caterpillar.* Cleveland, Ohio: Collins World, 1969.

———. *The Very Quiet Cricket.* New York: Putnam, 1990.

175

Word Recognition: Consonant *w*

Trivizas, Eugene. *The Three Little Wolves and the Big Bad Pig.* Illustrated by Helen Oxenbury. New York: Macmillan, 1993.

Grade levels: K–1.

The mother wolf informs her three young wolves that it is time they build their own house. They build a house of bricks, but the big bad pig comes along and tries to blow it down. He succeeds in destroying the house with a sledgehammer. So the wolves build a house of concrete. The big bad pig continues to destroy every house they build until they build one of flowers. The pig is so charmed by it that they all become friends.

Activities

1. Write the word *wolf* on the board. Ask the students to identify the word. Discuss how it begins with the letter *w*. Ask the students what word they would use when talking about more than one wolf. Write the word *wolves* on the board and then have the students read the title of the book. Have them speculate on what they think the story is about.

2. If the students are unfamiliar with the traditional story of the three little pigs, read any traditional version first.

3. Read aloud the story. Discuss how this story differs from the usual story of the three little pigs. Read the books by Steven Kellogg and Jon Scieszka, listed in the "Related books" section below. Discuss how they differ from the traditional versions. Talk about *Little Red Riding Hood* and the role that a wolf plays in that story. Do the students know of any other wolf stories?

4. Create a drawing of a wolf, leaving off the tail. Affix it to the wall. Give each student a piece of paper cut out in the shape of a wolf's tail. Tell them to choose a word that begins with the letter *w* and write the word on the tail. Play a version of pin the tail on the donkey, using the wolf instead. Leave on the wall the tails displayed with the *w* words.

Related books

George, Jean Craighead. *Look to the North: A Wolf Pup Diary.* Illustrated by Lucia Washburn. New York: HarperCollins, 1997.

Hyman, Trina Schart. *Little Red Riding Hood.* New York: Holiday House, 1983.

Kellogg, Steven. *The Three Little Pigs.* New York: Morrow, 1997.

Scieszka, Jon. *The True Story of the 3 Little Pigs.* Illustrated by Lane Smith. New York: Viking Penguin, 1989.

From: Bridges to Reading, Grades K–3: Teaching Reading Skills with Children's Literature. © 1999 Suzanne I. Barchers. Teacher Ideas Press (800) 237-6124.

Updike, John. *A Helpful Alphabet of Friendly Objects.* Photographs by David Updike. New York: Alfred A. Knopf, 1995.

Grade levels: K–1.

In this alphabet book, Updike provides poems about familiar objects from *A* to *Z*. Beginning with a photograph of a child eating an apple and ending with a discussion of weather at zero temperature, the treatment is clear and simple. Of course, a xylophone gets the nod for the letter *x*.

Activities

1. Because very few words begin with the letter *x,* many alphabet books use the word *xylophone* for the letter *x.* Yet the sound of *x* in *xylophone* is like that of the letter *z.* Therefore, this lesson will work best if a variety of alphabet books, such as those listed in the "Related books" section below, are used.

2. To begin the lesson, share Updike's alphabet book. Discuss how the word *xylophone* begins with the letter *x.* Then share Scott Gustafson's page on the letter *x.* (See his entry in the "Related books" section below.) Discuss the many uses of *x,* contrasting its sound in words such as *ox, excellent,* and *exciting.* Look in other alphabet books and compare how they use the letter *x.*

3. Look in the dictionary under the letter *x.* Do all the words that start with the letter *x* begin with the sound of the letter *z?*

4. Write the word *ox* on the board. Have the students think of rhyming words, such as *box, sox,* and *lox.* Think of other words that end in *x,* such as *fix, mix,* and *sax.* Put a box on a table. Label it "Our X Box." Have the students fill it with words containing the letter *x.*

Related books

Gustafson, Scott. *Alphabet Soup: A Feast of Letters.* Shelton, Conn.: The Greenwich Workshop, 1994.

Isadora, Rachel. *City Seen from A to Z.* New York: Trumpet, 1983.

Kitamura, Satoshi. *From Acorn to Zoo and Everything in Between in Alphabetical Order.* New York: Trumpet, 1992.

Mullins, Patricia. *V for Vanishing: An Alphabet of Endangered Animals.* New York: HarperCollins, 1993.

Ressmeyer, Roger. *Astronaut to Zodiac: A Young Stargazer's Alphabet.* New York: Crown, 1992.

Walker, John. *Ridiculous Rhymes from A to Z.* Illustrated by David Catrow. New York: Henry Holt, 1995.

From: Bridges to Reading, Grades K–3: Teaching Reading Skills with Children's Literature. © 1999 Suzanne I. Barchers. Teacher Ideas Press (800) 237-6124.

Word Recognition: Consonant *y*

Rashchka, Chris. *Yo! Yes!* New York: Orchard, 1993.

Grade levels: K–1.

Two boys who do not know each other meet on the street. The first boy begins the simple, but direct, conversation by saying "Yo!" The one boy confesses to having no fun because he has no friends. When the other boy suggests that he be a friend, they celebrate with a loud "Yow!"

Activities

1. This book provides ample opportunities for exploring basic words in addition to those beginning with the letter *y*. Begin by writing the word *yo* on the board. Ask the students what it means. Is it a traditional greeting or slang? Look it up in the dictionary.

2. Write the word *yes* on the board. Discuss how both words begin with the same letter. Can the students think of other words that begin with *y?*

3. Read the book aloud, allowing time for the students to enjoy the illustrations. As you are reading, discuss the body language of each of the boys. (If you want to demonstrate the importance of the illustrations, first read the book aloud without sharing the illustrations. Then read it again, showing the illustrations. Contrast the students' impressions of the book as they compare both experiences.)

4. Write all the different words that are used in the story on the board. How many begin with the letter *y?* Can the students think of other books containing very few words? Do they like books with simple text?

Related books

Aliki. *Hello! Good-bye!* New York: Greenwillow, 1996.

Kimmel, Eric A. *Baba Yaga: A Russian Folktale.* Illustrated by Megan Lloyd. New York: Holiday House, 1991.

Little, Mimi Otey. *Yoshiko and the Foreigner.* New York: Farrar, Straus & Giroux, 1996.

From: Bridges to Reading, Grades K–3: Teaching Reading Skills with Children's Literature. © 1999 Suzanne I. Barchers. Teacher Ideas Press (800) 237-6124.

From: Bridges to Reading, Grades K–3: Teaching Reading Skills with Children's Literature. © 1999 Suzanne I. Barchers. Teacher Ideas Press (800) 237-6124.

Gorog, Judith. *Zilla Sasparilla and the Mud Baby.* Illustrated by Amanda Harvey. Cambridge, Mass.: Candlewick Press, 1995.

Grade levels: K–1.

Zilla loses a shoe in the mud, and when she pulls it out, she also pulls out a mud baby. She takes the baby home, learning how to care for him so he will grow up like other children. Zilla worries that the river will one day reclaim him, and she makes plans to move away. But as they leave, she falls into the river. Her son jumps in and saves her, proving that the river couldn't harm him. They return home to live together happily.

Activities

1. Write the letter *z* on the board. Ask the students to name as many words as they can think of that start with *z*. Words they might think of include *zebra, zero, zigzag, zipper, zoo, zoom,* and *zone.*

2. Write the word *Zilla* on the board. Look it up in the dictionary and then discuss how the author invented the name. Discuss how *Zilla Sasparilla* sounds and look up the meaning of *sasparilla.*

3. Read the story aloud. Discuss the use of the name *Cinnamon* and how pleasant it sounds with *Zilla Sasparilla.* Do any of the students have unusual names? Ask them to ask their parents how they came to choose their names.

4. Several exotic-sounding place names begin with the letter *z*, for example, *Zabrze, Zacatecas, Zadar, Zagreb, Zama, Zambezi River, Zamboanga, Zante, Zanzibar, Zaporozhe, Zealand, Zeebrugge,* and *Zermatt.* Help the students find them on a map: Consult the dictionary for more places that begin with the letter *z*.

Related books

Calmenson, Stephanie. *Zip, Whiz, Zoom!* Illustrated by Dorothy Stott. Boston: Little, Brown, 1992.

Peet, Bill. *Zella, Zack, and Zodiac.* Boston: Houghton Mifflin, 1986.

London, Jonathan. *The Candystore Man.* Illustrated by Kevin O'Malley. New York: Lothrop, Lee and Shepard, 1998.

Grade levels: 2–3.

The candystore man can scoop ice cream, make a shake, give out penny candy, play the pinball machine, and give out treats to the football team. On Halloween, he's the Candystore King as he gives out candy to the trick-or-treaters. To round out his life, he plays the sax and writes and sings poetry. This lively story bounces with rhythm and rhyme.

Activities

1. This book offers many opportunities to use the context and illustrations to determine the meaning of any unknown words. Begin reading the story aloud. On the first page, hesitate before reading the words *dip* and *awake*. Ask the students to predict what the words might be. Then show them the text and discuss how the rhyme and context helped them choose the words, even without having heard the story before.

2. On the next set of pages, several words are printed in color: *fireballs, lollipops, jawbreakers, wax lips,* and *peppermint sticks.* Write the words on the board. Can the students read them easily? Then continue with the text. Discuss why the author illustrated the word *licorice whips* in black instead of in color as with the other words.

3. On the next set of pages, write the colored words on the board: *sh'bang, wallop, pop, bip-bop-shawak, slack.* Discuss the words and their possible meanings. Then read the page aloud. Discuss how the rhythm of the text improves when using made-up words.

4. Continue through the book in the same fashion, letting students anticipate words they might not know based on the context.

Related books

Andrews, Sylvia. *Rattlebone Rock.* Illustrated by Jennifer Plecas. New York: HarperCollins, 1995.

Barner, Bob. *Dem Bones.* San Francisco: Chronicle, 1996.

La Prise, Larry, Charles P. Macak, and Taftt Baker. *The Hokey Pokey.* Illustrated by Sheila Hamanaka. New York: Simon & Schuster, 1997.

Van Laan, Nancy. *Possum Come a-Knocking.* Illustrated by George Booth. New York: Alfred A. Knopf, 1990.

From: Bridges to Reading, Grades K-3: Teaching Reading Skills with Children's Literature. © 1999 Suzanne I. Barchers. Teacher Ideas Press (800) 237-6124.

Manning, Jane. *My First Songs.* New York: HarperCollins, 1998.

Grade levels: K–1.

This cheerful book contains 10 familiar songs for young singers: "The Wheels on the Bus," "Old MacDonald Had a Farm," "The Eentsy, Weentsy Spider," "Row, Row, Row Your Boat," "Ring Around the Rosie," "London Bridge," "Pop! Goes the Weasel," "Take Me Out to the Ball Game," "Hush, Little Baby," and "Twinkle, Twinkle, Little Star."

Activities

1. Begin by writing the words to "The Eentsy, Weentsy Spider" on the board or on chart paper. Teach the students the song. Ask them to look at the words to the song and find the words that appear most often. *The* appears in every line. Highlight *the* in each line by using colored chalk or a marker.

2. Tell the students you are going to try to trick them. They are to try to sing the song without saying the word *the*. Try it with them, pausing where you would say *the*. This is hard to do and will probably cause everyone to giggle. The next time, clap in place of each time you would singing the word *the*. Here, the students will be more successful. Remind them how important the word *the* is and that it is important to know how to spell it for their writing. Repeat the process with *and,* another word that appears frequently in the song.

3. At another class session, use "Hush, Little Baby" to teach *a* and *that* in the same fashion.

4. Just for fun, learn "London Bridge," acting out the words *down* and *up*.

5. Then learn "The Wheels on the Bus." Have the students make up additional verses. Write them out so that the students can practice reading them as they sing.

Related books

Okun, Milton, editor. *The Giant Book of Children's Songs.* Port Chester, N.Y.: Cherry Lane Music Company, 1993.

Pearson, Tracey Campbell. *Old MacDonald Had a Farm.* New York: Dial, 1984.

Rey, H. A. *Humpty Dumpty and other Mother Goose Songs.* New York: HarperCollins, 1943, 1971, 1995.

From: Bridges to Reading, Grades K-3: Teaching Reading Skills with Children's Literature. © 1999 Suzanne I. Barchers. Teacher Ideas Press (800) 237-6124.

Merriam, Eve. *A Sky Full of Poems.* Illustrated by Walter Gaffney-Kessell. New York: Dell, 1986.

Grade levels: 2–3.

This book should be required reading in every classroom. It is full of poems that celebrate wordplay, grammar, and the poetic process. Many of the poems use visual components, inspiring students to create their own concrete poetry.

Activities

1. Share the poem "Basic for Irresponsibility" on page 54. Discuss how the word *it* serves many purposes as a function word.

2. Choose one of the themes presented in this poem, such as the line, "IT is just the way things are." Create a riddle, building on this theme, using *it* frequently. For example,

    > IT happens everyday.
    > IT gets me started in the morning.
    > I don't like IT.
    > But I have to use IT.
    > IT is just the way things are.
    > What is IT?
    > (The alarm ringing.)

    Have the students create similar riddles, using the word *it.*

3. If the class is mature, read aloud "Basic for Further Irresponsibility" on page 55. The concept presented here is more difficult to grasp but is effective nonetheless. Discuss the use of *they* in the poem.

4. The poetry collections listed in the "Related books" section below contain many poems that are written in the first person. Share a number of them, then have the students create *I* poems.

Related books

Goldstein, Bobbye. *What's on the Menu?* Illustrated by Chris L. Demarest. New York: Puffin, 1992.

Prelutsky, Jack. *My Parents Think I'm Sleeping.* Illustrated by Yossi Abolafia. New York: Greenwillow, 1985.

———. *The New Kid on the Block.* Illustrated by James Stevenson. New York: Scholastic, 1984.

From: Bridges to Reading, Grades K–3: Teaching Reading Skills with Children's Literature. © 1999 Suzanne I. Barchers. Teacher Ideas Press (800) 237-6124.

Nodset, Joan L. *Go Away, Dog.* Illustrated by Paul Meisel. New York: HarperCollins, 1991, 1997.

Grade levels: K–1.

A little boy is playing when a dog joins him. He tells the dog to go away, asserting that he doesn't like him. Indeed, he doesn't like dogs at all. So he throws the stick to get the dog to leave, but the dog just returns. Soon the dog's tail wagging, rolling over, and loving personality win over the boy.

Activities

1. Begin reading this easy book aloud, stopping on page 17 to ask the students what they think will happen. Continue reading it, allowing the students to enjoy how the boy and dog become friends.

2. Write the words *go away* on the board. Have the students read the words. Then read the story again, having them raise their hands every time you read *go away.*

3. Ask the students what other words, phrases, or sentences were used frequently in the story. Write the sentences on the board, such as *I don't like you, dog.*

4. Discuss with the class how the little boy's voice probably changes at least four times in the story: when he tries to get the dog to leave, when he decides the dog is fun, when he tries to get the dog to leave again, and when he finally takes him home. Ask for four volunteers to read the different parts with the appropriate voice changes.

5. Choose a few of the words from the book, such as *shake, fun, dog,* and *wag.* Ask the students if they can think of words that rhyme with them. Write the word families on the board, reminding students that once they can read one word they can read many words just by changing the beginning letter.

Related books

Capucilli, Alyssa Satin. *Biscuit Finds a Friend.* Illustrated by Pat Schories. New York: HarperCollins, 1997.

Karlin, Nurit. *The Fat Cat Sat on the Mat.* New York: HarperCollins, 1996.

McGeorge, Constance W. *Boomer's Big Day.* Illustrated by Mary Whyte. San Francisco: Chronicle, 1994.

From: Bridges to Reading, Grades K–3: Teaching Reading Skills with Children's Literature. © 1999 Suzanne I. Barchers. Teacher Ideas Press (800) 237-6124.

Robart, Rose. *The Cake That Mack Ate.* Illustrated by Maryann Kovalski. Boston: Little, Brown, 1986.

Grade levels: 2–3.

The farmer's wife has baked a cake. This cumulative tale chronicles the sequence of making a cake, from the planting of seed for corn that fed the hen to the laying of the required egg. But, unfortunately, when the cake is ready for the birthday celebration, Mack the dog eats it.

Activities

1. When you read this book aloud, the students will not realize until the end that Mack, who ate the cake, is a dog. After reading the story, discuss the point at which the illustrator gives a hint that Mack is the dog who eats the cake and when it is confirmed.

2. Reread the story, having the students read along with you. They should be able to use the pictures to cue them to the first line on each page. The subsequent lines are repetitive.

3. Create new versions of the story by substituting a different food item. For example,

   > This is the pie that Mack ate. These are the apples that went into the pie that Mack ate. This is the tree that grew the apples, that went into the pie that Mack ate. This is the seed, that grew into the tree, that grew the apples, that went into the pie that Mack ate. This is the farmer who planted the seed, that grew into the tree, that grew the apples, that went into the pie that Mack ate. . . .

   Possible food variations include bread, a milk shake, pudding, or salad.

4. Have the students illustrate their new versions and keep them in the class library. Encourage the students to read the new versions during silent reading time.

Related books

Haas, Irene. *A Summertime Song.* New York: Simon & Schuster, 1997.

Hoff, Syd. *Happy Birthday, Danny and the Dinosaur!* New York: HarperCollins, 1995.

Spirn, Michele Sobel. *A Know-Nothing Birthday.* Illustrated by R. W. Alley. New York: HarperCollins, 1997.

From: Bridges to Reading, Grades K-3: Teaching Reading Skills with Children's Literature. © 1999 Suzanne I. Barchers. Teacher Ideas Press (800) 237-6124.

From: Bridges to Reading, Grades K–3: Teaching Reading Skills with Children's Literature. © 1999 Suzanne I. Barchers. Teacher Ideas Press (800) 237-6124.

Rader, Laura. *Chicken Little.* New York: HarperCollins, 1998.

Grade levels: K–1.

An acorn falls out of the sky, and Chicken Little thinks the sky is falling. She decides she must tell the king. On the way, she meets Henny Penny, Ducky Lucky, and Loosey Goosey. When they reach the king, he discovers the acorn and explains that it was an acorn that fell, not the sky.

Activities

1. Read the story aloud. Then list the names of all the animals on the board. Discuss how Henny Penny, Ducky Lucky, and Loosey Goosey are rhyming pairs. Add a third name to each, such as Henny Penny Lenny.

2. Write the word *king* on the board. Ask the students to think of all the words they can that rhyme with *king* (e.g., *bing, ching, ding, fling, ping, ring, sing, wing*). Explain that such a grouping is called a word family and that once they can read one of the words they can substitute the beginning consonant and easily read related words.

3. Identify the repeated sentences that occur throughout the book. Discuss the patterns. Then have the students read aloud the story with you.

4. Create a readers theatre script from the story by developing the narrator's part for moving along the action and using the spoken passages for the different characters. Have a group of students practice reading the script aloud and then share it with the class.

5. Compare this version with the version by Steven Kellogg listed in the "Related books" section below. How are they different?

Related books

Aardema, Verna. *This for That.* Illustrated by Victoria Chess. New York: Dial, 1997.

González, Lucía. *The Bossy Gallito.* Illustrated by Lulu Delacre. New York: Scholastic, 1994.

Kellogg, Steven. *Chicken Little.* New York: Morrow, 1988.

Zemach, Margot. *The Little Red Hen: An Old Story.* New York: Farrar, Straus & Giroux, 1983.

Barner, Bob. *Dem Bones.* San Francisco: Chronicle, 1996.

Grade levels: 2–3.

This familiar song highlights all the connections of the human skeleton. For each bone, text in a box gives scientific information. The illustrations of the skeletons are striking and humorous. The final spread shows a skeleton with the bones identified through a chart.

Activities

1. Read the dedication. Ask the students if they understand the humor in the dedication. After reading the book, discuss the dedication again for those who didn't understand the play on words.

2. First, read the main text. Then return to the beginning and read the information in the boxes. Many of the words may be unfamiliar to students, such as *clavicle*, *vertebrae*, and *scapula*. Write each of these words on the board. Have the students guess the pronunciations based on their knowledge of phonics. Use a dictionary to confirm the pronunciations.

3. Using large sheets of butcher paper, have the students work in pairs to draw outlines of their bodies. Have them sketch in their skeletal structure. Then have them label each of their bones, using the last spread in the book as a guide.

4. The 20 bones in this list represent only one-tenth of the bones an adult has. Have the students research other bones. Have each student identify a few of these bones on their skeletons.

5. For Halloween, repeat the process of researching the skeletal structure, only this time using a cat. Display drawings of labeled cat skeletons around the room.

Related books

Carle, Eric. *From Head to Toe.* New York: HarperCollins, 1997.

Culbertson, Roger, and Robert Margulies. *3-D Kid.* Illustrated by Robert Margulies. Paper engineering by Roger Culbertson. New York: W. H. Freeman, 1995.

Nikola-Lisa, W. *Shake dem Halloween Bones.* Illustrated by Mike Reed. Boston: Houghton Mifflin, 1997.

From: Bridges to Reading, Grades K–3: Teaching Reading Skills with Children's Literature. © 1999 Suzanne I. Barchers. Teacher Ideas Press (800) 237-6124.

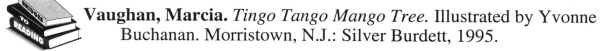

Vaughan, Marcia. *Tingo Tango Mango Tree.* Illustrated by Yvonne Buchanan. Morristown, N.J.: Silver Burdett, 1995.

Grade levels: K–1.

One day Sombala Bombala Rombala Roh, the iguana, finds a mango seed. She decides to plant it, setting out on a journey through the forest. After the mango tree grows, she needs help picking the mango. Various animals try, but it is the tiny bat that succeeds. The mango falls on the sleeping iguana's head, and when she awakes, she finds her mango has been eaten, leaving her another seed.

Activities

1. Read the story aloud. On the second reading, stop to write all the words with the short *a* sound on the board. Include the nonsense words, such as *pap,* and the names, such as *Nanaba Panaba Tanaba Goh.*

2. Discuss how the author makes up words, such as the names, using rhythm and rhyme. Make up a variety of words to rhyme with *mango*. Discuss how mango is made up of two small words: *man* and *go.* (Use the alphabet and add consonants, for example, *bango, cango, dango, fango.*) Write the words on the board and have the students read them with you.

3. Decide which one of the rhyming words would make a good name for a fruit. Using the song in the back of the book, sing it, substituting the new word for *mango.*

4. Challenge the students to make up new animal names that rhyme.

5. Use the story's unusual words, such as *calabash,* to continue to reinforce vowel sounds.

Related books

Baer, Gene. *THUMP, THUMP, Rat-a-Tat-Tat.* Illustrated by Lois Ehlert. New York: HarperCollins, 1989.

Karlin, Nurit. *The Fat Cat Sat on the Mat.* New York: HarperCollins, 1996.

Kimmel, Eric A. *The Gingerbread Man.* Illustrated by Megan Lloyd. New York: Holiday House, 1993.

Krudwig, Vickie Leigh. *Cucumber Soup.* Illustrated by Craig McFarland Brown. Golden, Colo.: Fulcrum, 1998.

Marshall, Janet. *Banana Moon.* New York: Greenwillow, 1998.

Robart, Rose. *The Cake That Mack Ate.* Illustrated by Maryann Kovalski. Boston: Little, Brown, 1986.

From: Bridges to Reading, Grades K–3: Teaching Reading Skills with Children's Literature. © 1999 Suzanne I. Barchers. Teacher Ideas Press (800) 237-6124.

Zemach, Margot. *The Little Red Hen: An Old Story.* New York: Farrar, Straus and Giroux, 1983.

Grade levels: K–1.

When the Little Red Hen finds a few grains of wheat, she decides to plant them. None of her friends will help, so she does it herself. As the wheat grows, she asks again who will help harvest, thresh, and take the wheat to be ground into flour. She bakes the bread herself, and when it is time to eat it, she shares it only with her chicks. Any version of this story can be used for the activities that follow.

Activities

1. Read the story aloud. Then write *Little Red Hen* on the board. Discuss how *little* has the short *i* sound and how both *red* and *hen* have the short *e* sound.

2. Read the story again and tell the students to be alert for other short *e* words: *well, fed, thresh.* When the students identify *friends,* include it, noting that the *i* is silent.

3. Brainstorm a list of rhyming words for *red* and *hen*. Have the students make up new sentences using the rhyming words. Emphasize that once they know *red* and *hen* they can remember all the rhyming words just by changing the first letter of the word.

4. Can the students think of two words that have *hen* in them? Discuss *when* and *then* and how the beginning changes with the additional letters. Mention that the students can remember how to read these words if they look for *hen* in them.

5. Have the students begin a word list, word wall, or word bank for short *e* words, adding to it as they come across new examples.

Related books

Baron, Alan. *Red Fox Dances.* Cambridge, Mass.: Candlewick Press, 1996.

Day, Alexandra. *Frank and Ernest.* New York: Scholastic, 1998.

Moncure, Jane Belk. *Word Bird Makes Words with Hen.* Illustrated by Linda Hohag. Mankato, Minn.: The Child's World, 1984.

Oppenheim, Joanne. *"Not Now!" Said the Cow.* Illustrated by Chris Demarest. New York: Bantam, 1989.

Patrick, Denise Lewis. *Red Dancing Shoes.* Illustrated by James E. Ransome. New York: Morrow, 1993.

From: Bridges to Reading, Grades K-3: Teaching Reading Skills with Children's Literature. © 1999 Suzanne I. Barchers. Teacher Ideas Press (800) 237-6124.

From: Bridges to Reading, Grades K-3: Teaching Reading Skills with Children's Literature. © 1999 Suzanne I. Barchers. Teacher Ideas Press (800) 237-6124.

Martin, David. *Little Chicken Chicken.* Illustrated by Sue Heap. Cambridge, Mass.: Candlewick Press, 1996.

Grade levels: K–1.

When Little Chicken Chicken, an imaginative fowl, finds a piece of string, she declares she is going to make a tightrope. The other chickens laugh at her, but she saves her string and other treasures she finds. When a thunderstorm comes, she performs for the others, earning their respect.

Activities

1. Write the title of the book on the board. Ask the students to read the title aloud. Discuss the sound of the short *i* in each of the words, explaining that they are going to be listening for words that have the sound they hear in words like *it*.

2. Read *Little Chicken Chicken* aloud. Encourage the students to join you each time you read her name aloud. List the names of the main characters on the board: *Little Chicken Chicken, Baby Chick, Rooster,* and the big chickens. Ask them to identify which one does not have the short *i* sound in it.

3. Write the word *chicken* on the board. Ask the students to write as many little words as they can using the letters in *chicken*. Some examples include *chick, hick, hi, hike, nick, neck, check, chink, ink, inch,* and *cinch.* How many can they find that have the short *i* sound?

4. Discuss the message of the story. Do the students ever get laughed at only to later set an example by following their dreams?

Related books

Baron, Alan. *Little Pig's Bouncy Ball.* Cambridge, Mass.: Candlewick Press, 1996.

Capucilli, Alyssa Satin. *Biscuit Finds a Friend.* Illustrated by Pat Schories. New York: HarperCollins, 1997.

Cohen, Caron Lee. *How Many Fish?* Illustrated by S. D. Schindler. New York: Harper-Collins, 1998.

Hutchins, Pat. *Little Pink Pig.* New York: Greenwillow, 1994.

Kellogg, Steven. *Chicken Little.* New York: Morrow, 1985.

Lobel, Arnold. *The Book of Pigericks.* New York: Harper & Row, 1983.

Rader, Laura. *Chicken Little.* New York: HarperCollins, 1998.

Walsh, Ellen Stoll. *Hop Jump.* New York: Trumpet, 1993.

Grade levels: K–1.

Betsy, a blue frog, observes that the other frogs come and go, hopping and jumping every time. She finds that she can't float like leaves, but she can twist and turn—dance! At first the other frogs are suspicious, but eventually all but one join in. Finally, they decide there is room for hopping *and* dancing.

Activities

1. Before reading the book aloud, write the word *frog* on the board. Ask the students what they think of when they think about frogs. Accept all reasonable answers. When someone mentions hopping or jumping, write *hop jump* on the board, explaining that the frogs in this story love to *hop jump* all the time. Ask if they would get tired of only walking instead of being able to run, jump, or skip.

2. Read the story aloud. On the second reading, have the students raise their hands every time they hear the word *hop*. Discuss how *frog* and *hop* both have the short *o* sound. What words can they think of that rhyme with *frog* and *hop?* Write their answers on the board.

3. Using blue chalk, draw a large blue oval on the board. Tell the students that this is the frog pond, another short *o* word. Tell them that they are going to try to fill the pond up with additional short *o* words. Ask each student to think of one and let them take turns writing it in the pond.

4. For a variation, give each student a piece of blue construction paper. Have them cut out a large oval. Label it with the word *pond.* Then allow the students to fill in their own ponds with short *o* words.

Related books

Andrews, Sylvia. *Rattlebone Rock.* Illustrated by Jennifer Plecas. New York: HarperCollins, 1995.

Baron, Alan. *Red Fox Dances.* Cambridge, Mass.: Candlewick Press, 1996.

Marshall, James. *Fox on the Job.* New York: Trumpet, 1988.

Murphy, Stuart J. *Ready, Set, Hop!* Illustrated by Jon Buller. New York: HarperCollins, 1996.

Nielsen, Shelly. *Fun with O/o.* Minneapolis, Minn.: Abdo & Daughters, 1992.

From: Bridges to Reading, Grades K–3: Teaching Reading Skills with Children's Literature. © 1999 Suzanne I. Barchers. Teacher Ideas Press (800) 237-6124.

From: Bridges to Reading, Grades K-3: Teaching Reading Skills with Children's Literature. © 1999 Suzanne I. Barchers. Teacher Ideas Press (800) 237-6124.

Edwards, Pamela Duncan. _Some Smug Slug._ Illustrated by Henry Cole. New York: HarperCollins, 1996.

Grade levels: K–1.

A slug starts on a journey. Various creatures warn her to stop, but she continues to saunter and swagger along. While others observe her folly, she shambles on, higher and higher. Finally, she reaches the summit, where she becomes a succulent snack. The alliteration and use of many words with the short _u_ sound make this an entertaining book.

Activities

1. Ask the students how many have seen a slug. If they are not common in your location, try to get photographs of real slugs. Share the photographs, discussing how slugs leave slime behind them. Discuss how people try to get rid of these pests because of the damage they can do to gardens and plants. For example, in some areas, people shake salt on them. Because they are made up primarily of water, the salt shrivels the slugs, killing them.

2. Write the title of the story on the board. Ask the students what vowel sound they hear in each word. Point out that the word _some_ has the same vowel sound as _smug_ and _slug_, even though it has an _o_ for the vowel. Can they think of words that rhyme with _smug_ and _slug?_

3. Read the story aloud. Periodically ask the students if they can guess why the other creatures try to dissuade the slug from continuing. Are they surprised by the ending?

4. Read the story again. Ask the students to raise their hands when they hear other words that have the short _u_ sound. Write the words on the board. Can they think of other words the author might have used?

Related books

Baer, Gene. _THUMP, THUMP, Rat-a-Tat-Tat._ Illustrated by Lois Ehlert. New York: HarperCollins, 1989.

Egielski, Richard. _Buz._ New York: HarperCollins, 1995.

Nielsen, Shelly. _Fun with U/u._ Minneapolis, Minn.: Abdo & Daughters, 1992.

Walsh, Ellen Stoll. _Hop Jump._ New York: Trumpet, 1993.

West, Colin. _"Buzz, Buzz, Buzz," Went Bumblebee._ Cambridge, Mass.: Candlewick Press, 1996.

Schroeder, Pamela J. P., and Jean M. Donisch. *What's the Big Idea? Shapes.* Vero Beach, Fla.: Rourke, 1996.

Grade levels: K–1.

Each double-page spread illustrates and discusses a shape: circle, square, triangle, rectangle, oval, diamond, polygon, parallelogram, trapezoid, heart, and star. The illustrations show a variety of items with that shape. Includes a glossary and a section of suggestions for using shapes.

Activities

1. Share the book, discussing the items that are pictured for each shape. Omit the more difficult shapes if the students have not yet learned the basic shapes.

2. Return to the book and ask volunteers to point out the words that name the shapes. Write the words on the board. Discuss the beginning and ending letters for each word.

3. Give each student a 9 x 9 inch piece of construction paper and a pencil. Tell them to listen carefully while you give them directions to follow. Give the following directions:

   > Place the paper in front of you.
   > Fold the paper in half.
   > Open the paper up.
   > Fold the paper again the other way. You should have four squares.
   > In the square in the upper left, draw one big circle.
   > In the square in the upper right, draw a line from one corner to the next.
   > In the square in the lower left, draw a vertical line through the middle of the square.
   > In the square in the lower right, draw an oval.

4. Have the students repeat back to you the directions while you draw the same diagram on the board as they should have on their paper. Then label the shapes in the four squares. Have the students copy the names of the shapes into the squares. Repeat with the other shapes, if desired.

From: Bridges to Reading, Grades K–3: Teaching Reading Skills with Children's Literature. © 1999 Suzanne I. Barchers. Teacher Ideas Press (800) 237-6124.

Related books

Dodds, Dayle Ann. *The Shape of Things.* Illustrated by Julie Lacome. Cambridge, Mass.: Candlewick Press, 1994.

Grover, Max. *Circles and Squares Everywhere!* San Diego, Calif.: Harcourt Brace & Company, 1996.

Murphy, Stuart J. *Circus Shapes.* Illustrated by Edward Miller. New York: HarperCollins, 1998.

Schaefer, Carole Lexa. *The Squiggle.* Illustrated by Pierr Morgan. New York: Crown, 1996.

Wheeler, Cindy. *More Simple Signs.* New York: Viking, 1998.

From: Bridges to Reading, Grades K–3: Teaching Reading Skills with Children's Literature. © 1999 Suzanne I. Barchers. Teacher Ideas Press (800) 237-6124.

Schroeder, Pamela J. P., and Jean M. Donisch. *What's the Big Idea? Time.* Vero Beach, Fla.: Rourke, 1996.

Grade levels: 2–3.

Readers can explore a variety of time-related concepts through pictures and simple text. Beginning with a discussion of what time is, the book discusses seconds, minutes, hours, day and night, a week, a month, a year, before and after, young and old, and special times. A glossary and additional ideas about time conclude the book.

Activities

1. Begin by asking students what time they got up that morning. Can they recall what time they had breakfast, left for school, and arrived at school? Do they have their own alarm clock or do they rely on siblings or adults to keep them on schedule?

2. Brainstorm all the words they can think of that have to do with time. Write them on the board. Read the book aloud. Then ask the students what words they would add to the list on the board.

3. Create a word wall or bulletin board entitled "It's About Time." Begin the wall by having students copy the words from the list onto cards, affixing them to the wall. Then work together to create a weeklong schedule, showing the times for various activities throughout the day. Add it to the word wall.

4. Have the students use their journal to keep track of a typical day. Have them record the time when they get up, eat breakfast, and leave for school, continuing the process until they go to bed that night. Have them complete the log during the weekend. Analyze how much time they spend in various activities, such as playing games, watching television, and doing homework. Can they find ways to use time more efficiently?

Related books

Grossman, Bill. *The Guy Who Was Five Minutes Late.* Illustrated by Judy Glasser. New York: Harper & Row, 1990.

Murphy, Stuart J. *Get Up and Go!* Illustrated by Diane Greenseid. New York: HarperCollins, 1996.

Wheeler, Cindy. *More Simple Signs.* New York: Viking, 1998.

From: Bridges to Reading, Grades K–3: Teaching Reading Skills with Children's Literature. © 1999 Suzanne I. Barchers. Teacher Ideas Press (800) 237-6124.

From: Bridges to Reading, Grades K-3: Teaching Reading Skills with Children's Literature. © 1999 Suzanne I. Barchers. Teacher Ideas Press (800) 237-6124.

The following books can be used to teach a variety of vowel sounds using any of the preceding methods.

Long *a*

Hennessy, B. G. *Jake Baked the Cake.* Illustrated by Mary Morgan. New York: Penguin, 1990.

Merriam, Eve. *Train Leaves the Station.* Illustrated by Dave Gottlieb. New York: Trumpet, 1988.

Robart, Rose. *The Cake That Mack Ate.* Illustrated by Maryann Kovalski. Boston: Little, Brown, 1986.

Long *ar*

Jeram, Anita. *Contrary Mary.* Cambridge, Mass.: Candlewick Press, 1995.

———. *Daisy Dare.* Cambridge, Mass.: Candlewick Press, 1995.

Long *e*

Barton, Byron. *The Wee Little Woman.* New York: HarperCollins, 1995.

MacDonald, Margaret Read. *Pickin' Peas.* Illustrated by Pat Cummings. New York: HarperCollins, 1998.

Shaw, Nancy. *Sheep in a Jeep.* Illustrated by Margot Apple. Boston: Houghton Mifflin, 1986.

———. *Sheep Out to Eat.* Illustrated by Margot Apple. Boston: Houghton Mifflin, 1992.

Long *i*

Hayes, Sarah. *Nine Ducks Nine.* New York: HarperCollins, 1996.

Yorinks, Arthur. *Whitefish Will Rides Again.* Illustrated by Mort Drucker. New York: HarperCollins, 1994.

Long *o*

Oppenheim, Joanne. *"Not Now!" Said the Cow.* Illustrated by Chris Demarest. New York: Bantam, 1989.

Vaughan, Marcia. *Tingo Tango Mango Tree.* Illustrated by Yvonne Buchanan. Morristown, N.J.: Silver Burdett, 1995.

West, Colin. *"Only Joking!" Laughed the Lobster.* Cambridge, Mass.: Candlewick Press, 1995.

Bibliography of Vowel Sounds

Long *u*

Eversole, Robyn. *The Flute Player.* Illustrated by G. Brian Karas. New York: Orchard, 1995.

Ew

Gershator, Phyllis. *Tukama Tootles the Flute.* Illustrated by Synthia Saint James. New York: Orchard, 1994.

Numeroff, Laura, and Barney Saltzberg. *Two for Stew.* Illustrated by Salvatore Murdocca. New York: Simon & Schuster, 1996.

Ow

McBratney, Sam. *The Caterpillow Fight.* Cambridge, Mass.: Candlewick Press, 1996.

Various Vowels

Grossman, Bill. *The Banging Book.* Illustrated by Robert Zimmerman. New York: HarperCollins, 1995.

Marshall, Janet. *Banana Moon.* New York: Greenwillow, 1998.

From: Bridges to Reading, Grades K-3: Teaching Reading Skills with Children's Literature. © 1999 Suzanne I. Barchers. Teacher Ideas Press (800) 237-6124.

Index of Authors and Titles

Index of Authors and Titles

Suzanne I. Barchers received her bachelor of science degree in elementary education from Eastern Illinois University, her master's degree in education in reading from Oregon State University, and her doctor of education degree in curriculum and instruction from the University of Colorado, Boulder.

After 15 years as a teacher and administrator in public and private schools, Suzanne began a writing and editing career. She has published more than 15 books, including college textbooks and the award-winning *Wise Women: Folk and Fairy Tales from Around the World* (Libraries Unlimited). She also co-authored *Cooking Up World History*, 2d ed. (Teacher Ideas Press, 1999).

Suzanne has two adult sons and currently resides in Arvada, Colorado, with her husband, Dan. She teaches children's literature at the University of Colorado, Denver, and continues her writing and editing career.